B IS FOR BALLROOM

Be your own armchair dance-floor expert

ANTON DU BEKE

EDITED BY

Natasha Garnett

Constable • London

Constable & Robinson Ltd
55–56 Russell Square
London WC1B 4HP
www.constablerobinson.com

First published in the UK by Constable,
an imprint of Constable & Robinson Ltd., 2012

A copy of the British Library Cataloguing in
Publication data is available from the British Library

ISBN 978-1-47210-068-9 (hardback)
ISBN 978-1-47210-257-7 (ebook)

Printed and bound in the UK

1 3 5 7 9 10 8 6 4 2

MIX
Paper from
responsible sources
FSC® C018072

For anyone who loves a bit of dancing.
Even those who have simply just thought about it
but never got round to it.

Also by Anton du Beke
Anton's Dance Class

ACKNOWLEDGEMENTS

I would like to thank a troupe of people for making this book possible: the great Gordon Wise at Curtis Brown and the magnificent team at Constable & Robinson, with special thanks to my editor Andreas Campomar, who went out of his way to make this book sparkle, and Natasha Garnett, who helped me to choreograph the book.

And lastly and most importantly of all I would like to thank my long-suffering dance partner Erin Boag. It really does take two to tango – and she would know.

ENTRANCE

Ladies and gentlemen, boys and girls, I hope you are in the mood for dancing, because I am about to take your hand, lead you to the floor and introduce you to the spectacular, fabulous and dazzling world of ballroom dance.

In my capacity as a professional dancer I am going to guide you step by step through everything you need to know. I will introduce you to the dances, teach you technique and verse you in all that tricky terminology. We are going to quickstep our way through the history of ballroom, partner up with some of the more colourful characters – past and present – on the scene, and waltz through some of the great stories and anecdotes about this wonderful pastime. And we are going to do all this without you having to take a single class, break a leg, have me drag you across the floor or even leave the comfort of your armchair.

It goes without saying that ballroom dancing is enjoying something of a revival at the moment. Dance schools and classes the length and breadth of the country are filling up with students of all ages keen to get to grips with the Tango – and with their partner in the process – or to master the art of the Waltz. Tours featuring professional dancers sell out overnight, and television dance shows have become must-see events for the entire family with record numbers of viewers not only in the UK and US but around the world from Australia to South Korea. Ballroom dancing, with its sequins, spandex and spangles, its big band music and its dramas on and off the dance floor, has never been so popular, I'm glad to say – otherwise I'd be out of a job!

Why has it become so popular? Well, the simple reason, to my mind, is that it is just so much fun. It's entertaining, it's lively and it's exhilarating both to perform and to watch. It puts a smile on people's faces and that's what we all need in these difficult times.

Now, just as you don't need to be Roger Federer to enjoy tennis, or David Beckham to understand the offside rule, or Darcey Bussell to know what a plié is, you don't need to be able to dance well to appreciate ballroom. In fact, you don't need be able to dance at all.

I know there are a great many of you out there who can't get your head – or perhaps more importantly your feet – round footwork; who don't do posture, let alone poise; and who, when it comes to timing, struggle even when it comes to boiling an egg. Lord knows, I've partnered enough of you in my time. But that's not to say that you can't enjoy and know a thing or two about the subject, and at the very least become your very own armchair aficionado. Some of you may go to the many ballroom competitions, formal or informal, on the circuit or in your neighbourhood; for others the extent of your passion may be sitting down for a regular fix of your favourite dance show, waving your imaginary paddles in your hands when the scores come in; or maybe you like to see it performed live in a wonderful stage spectacular; you may even already be a bit of a dancer yourself. Whichever you are, stay with me, in hold as we say, because I am about to unlock all the secrets of ballroom dance.

If you want to know your Botafogo from your fleckle, have ever wondered how the Foxtrot got its name or questioned why the Quickstep is so quick, then this is the book for you. We're going to see what the judges in all the dance competitions look for in each of the dances, find out why they always seem to be so obsessed with the dancers' hands when surely they should be looking at their feet, and discover why they get so hot under the collar when it comes to lifts. We're also going to look at the sequins and swirls of costumes, see where the first dances came from and find out why there can be too many capes in a Paso Doble.

My aim is to answer all the questions you've ever wanted to know about ballroom but were afraid to ask, and to introduce you to this magical, beautiful and sometimes rather bizarre world that I have been fortunate enough to be part of for nearly thirty years now.

My own fascination with ballroom began in a church hall in my hometown of Sevenoaks, Kent, when I was just a lad of fourteen. I'd been sent by my mother to collect my sister Veronica from a local dance class, which she attended every week. Now, up until that point in time I think it would be safe to say that I had never been interested in dance. Like most boys my age all I really cared about was football and I thought that boys who danced were, frankly, rather wet. But when I walked into that room for the first time my opinion quickly changed.

There I was, a lone teenage boy surrounded by a group of lovely young girls. The lesson was still in progress and I suddenly found myself being roped in to help with a routine. I was a reluctant participant at first, but as the girls clamoured for me to partner them, I thought 'This isn't so bad after all.' Shameless, I know, but I'd never had much luck with the girls prior to that moment.

But it wasn't just the girls that held my attention that evening. I was fascinated by the discipline of the dance itself: the routines, the technique, the poise and the holds. And I realized there and then that this was not only a rather jolly way of whiling away an evening, but something that I might be good at if I gave it a try. It was a defining moment in my life and from that moment on I never looked back. I went on to enrol in weekly classes, took it a step further when I started to compete as an amateur, and then further still when eventually I turned professional and made it my career.

Over the years I have taught many people to dance, either one on one or in classes — and let's not forget those celebrities in front of the camera! I have shown each of my pupils the ropes with the aim not only of transforming them into credible dancers, but of sharing with them my knowledge, experience and love of ballroom. And now I want to do the same with you — even if you don't want to reach for your dancing shoes.

So this is my quickstep-by-quickstep guide to ballroom dancing. To learn more about this fascinating world, simply flip over the page, and we'll take a turn together.

A IS FOR ...

ALIGNMENT

This is where it all begins. Without alignment you can't start dancing! Alignment is all about where you and your partner are pointing and which way you are going. If you go one way and I go another – well, that's simply not ballroom. We might as well sit the next dance out.

Because you and your partner are in such close proximity, in what we call a 'closed hold position', you need to have chosen your direction and got yourself aligned in order to move across the floor in harmony. Whether you are going diagonally towards the wall, down the line of the dance floor, dancing around the room in a clockwise fashion or dancing 'to centre', you always need be moving together. This is one of the first things that any judge will be looking for. If you haven't mastered the art of alignment you will either end up disappearing up each other's armpits or in a tangled mess on the floor, which isn't the look you're aiming for.

The man is always the leader in ballroom and it's his

job to set up the alignment and make the correct choice of direction for the steps you make once you are on the floor. Ladies, I know that might sound old-fashioned in this day and age, but I'm afraid that's how it works in competitive dance. If you and your partner are the type of couple prone to rowing in the car while struggling with the map when your Sat Nav isn't working, then you might think ballroom is not for you. But luckily, ballroom dancing is easier than life. Just surrender yourself to the notion of alignment, clasp each other in a tender embrace (not too tender, mind) learn a few simple rules and you'll be well on your way to ballroom brilliance.

AMERICAN SMOOTH

I can't help but love an American Smooth. It's wonderfully stylish, fun to dance and a joy to watch. But armchair aficionados take note: despite the fact that it features in many television dance shows, it is not actually one of the standardized ballroom dances, and would never feature in a competition. It's simply a style of dance – or what I like to call a number.

Hailing from America, as its name obviously suggests, this style of dance first debuted on music hall stages across the pond at beginning of the last century, and then became immensely popular in musical theatre on Broadway and in London's West End. But it's really thanks to Hollywood that this style of dance took off. Think Fred Astaire and Ginger Rogers, or the late, great Gene Kelly. Think movies like *Top Hat* or *Singin' in the Rain*. That's why we all know and love it so much.

You want to be dancing the American Smooth to those classic, old-time romantic numbers. Songs by Cole Porter, the composer Jerome Kern or the great American songwriter Irving Berlin are perfect. Berlin's magical tunes 'It Only Happens When I Dance With You' or 'Cheek to Cheek' happen to be my favourite pieces of music to dance the American Smooth to. It's all about floaty frocks, top hat and tails, and conjuring up a sense of enchantment.

Now the reason why the American Smooth doesn't qualify as a standardized competitive dance is down to the fact that you are not always in the hold position — which is the golden rule of ballroom, as opposed to Latin, dancing. In the American Smooth you and your partner can have a little time off from one another. You might be in hold for a minute, break off, dance apart, do your own thing for a moment or two, add bits here and there, tap, turn and then come back together to do a little ballroom or even attempt a lift or two. It's these crowd-pleasing moves – the pivots, the twirls, the spins and especially the lifts, because we all love one of those – that make this style of dance so popular.

The American Smooth may not feature in competition dancing, but it is often included on television dance shows because it's so entertaining. Although it's what a professional would call 'unstandardized', it looks just wonderful and is a real pleasure to dance, even if they won't let you win the World Championships with it.

My professional partner Erin Boag took to the floor with the athlete Colin Jackson on Strictly Come Dancing and they dazzled everyone with their dizzying American Smooth routine. And I'm rather fond of it myself for those little moments when I can pop off on my own and do my thing with a top hat (positioned at a jaunty angle, of course) and a cane – before I rejoin my partner. I love that.

There are some grandees in the ballroom world who are rather snobbish about the American Smooth. Even my old dance teacher looked on it with a degree of disdain, declaring that it was 'danced by people who can't do ballroom properly' but I have to say I disagree. It's a miscellany of all that's great about dance: a number that can be performed to an array of tempos – fast or slow; full of character, acting, bounce and happiness. Whether

I am dancing it myself or just watching, it always brings a smile to my face.

The American Smooth has another advantage, which is that you don't have to touch your partner for too long if you don't want to. Very useful if they are getting on your nerves! So if she has a propensity to step on your toes, or he's getting over-familiar with his hands try this one out, because you can keep each other at arm's length when you've had enough.

AMERICAN SPIN

This one's for you, ladies. The American Spin is what we call a 'variation', which occurs in the Jive. For those of you struggling with your dance terminology, a variation is simply a combination of three or more individual steps. Think of it as a group of letters: when these are positioned in a certain way they may make up a specific word; muddle them up again and you'll have another word – a bit like an anagram – and each different combination will give you a new (or varying) sequence.

So the American Spin is a variation that we do in the Jive and it's really just a spin on the right foot for the girls. She makes a 360-degree turn on her foot, and that makes one American Spin. But obviously, this being a variation, it consists of more than just that, and both partners need to set themselves up for the lady's spin.

You can have a single spin, a double one or even a triple, if you are feeling very footsure and up for a little giddiness. If she hits a triple American Spin, she will have spun like a top. It's a tricky move to pull off and probably best not attempted if you've indulged in a tipple or two before taking to the floor.

However, an American Spin is a wonderful little showpiece to behold if mastered correctly, and there will be much applause once the lady has come full circle. And gentlemen, before you go and sulk on the side of the dance floor because your girl is getting all the glory, know too that you have an important role to play in the American Spin: you are there to set it all up and give her the strength, support and balance that she needs to get that spin going. And most important of all, you're there to catch her, because remember, a badly caught woman is a furious woman!

★ ★ ★

ARGENTINE TANGO

For those of you wanting lots of contact with your partner, a good dance to try is the Argentine Tango. But before we get any further tangled up I need to address a couple of misconceptions about this dance. The Tango as we know and love it is a very distinctive dance, one that we are all familiar with thanks to its vibrancy, intensity and sheer passion. We think of couples pacing dramatically across the floor together, their legs snaking around each other, their heels flicking. He's all spurs and chaps, she's in a tight little number cut away to reveal a glimpse of thigh, with a flower in her hair, scarf round her neck and rose clamped between her teeth, and that's the Tango – well, a pastiche of it anyway.

But when we talk about Tango in ballroom we aren't referring to the Argentine Tango, even though that's the ancestor of what we see in competitive dancing today. The modern Tango is a more refined, choreographed dance and has become one of the classic, standardized ballroom dances. So it has a slightly higher status these days than its Latin cousin, but that doesn't mean the Argentine Tango isn't worthy of an entry in this book. If anything it has a far more interesting and racy history.

The Argentine Tango has been around for hundreds

of years and was first developed in Buenos Aires. In its earliest form it was a simple dance developed by West Indian and Cuban immigrants. By the 1870s it had become more sophisticated in style and content. Back then it was called the Milonga, and it went on to become hugely popular throughout Argentina and Uruguay. In time, the Argentine Tango came to be embraced by high society all over Latin America before travelling to Europe and becoming fashionable there.

This was the dance of the gauchos, who on their return from the plains would hit the nearest salons, seeking both refreshment and company – and, to put it politely, they were happy to pay for both. Caked in sweat from their horses and their day's work and still wearing their chaps and muddy riding boots, they might not have made the most fragrant dancing partners but this didn't dissuade the girls, especially when there was money to be made.

The Argentine Tango was a dance of two parts. First, because the men outnumbered the women, the men would dance a form of duel in order to see who would get the girl. Once a dancer had won her he would lead her on to the floor for a fiery, frisson-filled dance. And it was because of the fact that the men were still in their riding gear that the Tango is performed quite 'high', even today – torso to torso, with the bottom halves of the two bodies kept apart. The idea is to lean forward into one another. The lady holds her head back and to the left – no doubt originally to avoid the smell of her partner – with her face to the left as she leans into his chest. So the contact and the intimacy is all at the top, while downstairs we now have room for all that kicking and entwinement of the legs as they suggestively rub up and down one another. Some call that 'decoration', but I think I could find another word for it. Certainly back then, everyone knew what was going on, not least because money was being exchanged. I'm glad to say that that's something that has changed, but to this day it's a very sexy, sensual and intimate dance, one in which the man has complete control over the woman. And if you're a good enough tango-er, she's not going to complain.

I love the passion of this dance, and when you see it performed by true experts – such as Flavia Cacace and Vincent Simone – it really is quite thrilling to watch. I've danced it myself many, many times over the years – though never on television. 'Why?' I hear you ask. Because, being a more advanced dance, in television contests they tend to put the Argentine Tango quite late in the series – perhaps as late as the semi-finals. Reader, I hate to admit this, but I have never once got that far in a TV dance show. I get to the brink, and then my partner and I are out, and the Argentine Tango is forever beyond my grasp.

This really is a dance of intimacy, so if you want to get your pulse racing with someone in particular, this could be your dance. When it comes to selecting music, my tip is to stick to authentic tunes so that the rhythm and tempo are right; I think you can't go wrong with anything by the great Argentine composer Astor Piazzolla, who really was the King of Tango. And my advice would also be to cut out some of the more elaborate kicks at first. You don't want to injure yourself on your first night. Start slowly, don't get too excited and build it up. And lads, as much as you might want to get into the spirit of the original dance, remember that you're not a gaucho out on the South American pampas, so have a shower, wear a nice aftershave and don't whatever you do offer your lady friend any money!

ASTAIRE, FRED

'The history of dance on film begins with Astaire,' said Gene Kelly about his fellow film star, and on that point I am in agreement. As far as I am concerned Astaire was a genius. Although he was not a 'ballroom dancer' in the sense that he never competed, he was the first and arguably the best of the great dance entertainers, and his influence and impact were vast. He has a long and varied list of admirers, including both Rudolf Nureyev and Mikhail Baryshnikov, the celebrated choreographer George Balanchine and the magical entertainer Sammy Davis Jr. Even Michael Jackson was said to have been such a fan of his that he would watch Astaire's films over and over again, seeking inspiration for his own routines.

In the course of a career that would span over seventy years, Astaire went on to become not only a leading figure on the stages of Broadway and the West End but also to star in 31 Hollywood musical films, from *Top Hat* and *Funny Face* to *The Gay Divorcee*, in which, despite his humble protestations that he couldn't sing, he mesmerized his audience with his enchanting song and dance routine to Cole Porter's 'Night and Day'.

Born in 1899 in Nebraska, Omaha, as a young child Astaire never had any desire to become a dancer. In fact the real star of the family when it came to fancy footwork was his older sister Adele, who took frequent classes and loved to perform. But Astaire's mother, who had aspirations for her children, realized that he had potential and encouraged the siblings to form a brother-and-sister Vaudeville act, popular in the music halls at the time. As the pair started working together and gained something of a reputation it wasn't long before the family upped sticks and moved to New York. The

Astaire children subsequently gained a huge following with their slapstick routines, which often involved young Fred performing dressed in what would become his signature look of top hat and tails – only to change into a lobster outfit for the second act of the routine. Initially, Adele was considered the more gifted of the pair, but as the years passed Fred found his feet and became the one to watch. Despite their success both on Broadway and the London stage the partnership came to an end when Adele married into the British aristocracy, having started stepping out with Lord Charles Cavendish, son of the Duke of Devonshire.

It didn't take long for Astaire to find himself a new partner, especially once a career in Hollywood beckoned – even if the report for his first screen test was less than promising: 'Can't act. Can't sing. Balding. But can dance a little.' Astaire went on to prove all his critics wrong, and in the course of his film career partnered some of the most celebrated Hollywood actresses of the age: Rita Hayworth; the tap dancing geniuses that were Ann Miller and Eleanor Powell; Leslie Caron; Judy Garland and the classically trained Cyd Charisse. He made each and every one of them look like a goddess. That was his skill and they loved him for it, but of course his greatest and most memorable partnership was with Ginger Rogers. The on-screen chemistry of the pair –

the tension, comedy and art between them – became so popular with audiences that they went on to make ten movies together, from *Flying Down to Rio* to *Shall We Dance*.

What made Astaire such a great dancer was that there was a marvellous looseness about him, a wonderful poise and a fine swagger. He never made any woman who danced with him look uncomfortable, no matter what their ability level, height, size or style. And he also looked pretty damned good in a suit too – not that he would like to be remembered for his sartorial style. He once complained that 'people think I was born in a top hat and tails', adding that he would be happy never to wear that particular get-up again in his life.

B IS FOR ...

BALLROOM DANCE

So how do we define the beautiful recreation that is ballroom dancing? Well, the way I like to describe it is two partners moving in such perfect harmony together that they are dancing as one. That's the essence of it and that's what differentiates it from other forms of dance. In hold you communicate with one another through your bodies but never with eye contact, and this is the key difference between ballroom dancing and the form known as Latin, where you dance separately but keep your eyes fixed on one another. In Latin you are much further apart, which I have always found slightly bizarre given the steaminess of the Latin American dances. But aside from that the two forms have strong similarities in that they both require balance, posture, timing and line – which is why when we talk about 'ballroom' they fall under the same umbrella. To avoid confusion some people refer to ballroom as 'standard', but being rather an old-fashioned type of chap I'm afraid I wholly disapprove of that – in fact I'd rather chop off my left foot than use the word 'standard' in this way. Which goes to show how strongly I feel, because I wouldn't be much good on the dance floor after that.

Rant over. What you need to know is that there are ten standardized dances in competitive ballroom dancing and these are as follows: the Foxtrot, the Waltz, the Viennese Waltz, the Quickstep, the Jive, the Samba, the Cha-cha-cha, the Tango, the Rumba and the Paso Doble. These are then subdivided into the ballroom and Latin categories. 'Which is easier?' you might ask. Well, that really depends on your strengths and weaknesses as a dancer, but you need to be able to master both if you are going to do well in a competition.

We will talk about Latin dance later on, but for now I want to concentrate on ballroom. In true ballroom, because the couple are always in hold – and with any luck are dancing in time to the music and in step with one another – their two bodies should appear to be as one as they sweep across the floor. They should give the overall impression that they are simply being carried along. That's the goal to aim for in ballroom dance.

The word 'ballroom' has its origins in the Latin word ballare, which literally means 'to dance'; we've been doing ballroom dancing for centuries. Long before we started dancing competitively, before we had sequins and glitter balls, it was a prime social activity. It appeared in Europe towards the end of the sixteenth century in the midst of the Renaissance, and back in those days it was a more refined version of the folk dance. At first it was a style of dance that belonged to the privileged classes as they socialized – leaving the rest of us commoners to our folksy ways – but over a short period of time that changed and those boundaries, thankfully, became blurred. Of course, our ancestors weren't foxtrotting or quickstepping back then, and wouldn't be for another four centuries, but they had their own sequences to keep them entertained. They danced the Minuet together or the Quadrille; there was the Polonaise, the Mazurka and the Polka. All of them are really rather beautiful to behold but have been long out of fashion – so much so that we refer to them these days as 'historical dances'.

The dances may have changed over the years as music, culture, fashions and social history evolved but the essence of ballroom remains the same: man dancing with woman in close proximity, heads looking away, sweeping and swinging, gliding around the floor, moving as one, body to body. I can't imagine why I took this up as a profession – pressing up against girls all day and most of the night. I hate my job.

BALLROOMS

I'm a great believer in having a dance where and when the mood takes you, whether you fancy a little twirl round your kitchen on a Saturday night with the missus, a quick little chassé or two to fill in those dreary moments waiting for the bus, or even a song and a dance in the rain à la Gene Kelly. I've even been known to do a quick pivot turn or two round the ninth hole on the golf course – when no one is looking, of course, as I am not sure it complies with the club rules. We've been dancing since the beginning of time and have always found a space for this very special social pursuit. We've been dancing round fires, in woods and fields and in medieval buildings, halls, social clubs and theatres. It doesn't matter who we are or where we come from – we've always found a way to express ourselves through dance and have a jolly good knees-up.

In the eighteenth century we got a little more sophisticated, and as dance became increasingly popular we decided that we should start creating specially designated spaces where we could congregate to sweep each other off our feet. And so, taking our lead from the courts of Europe, we set about building public ballrooms.

The ballrooms of the European royal courts were

terrifically opulent, magnificent affairs. This was where the grandest folk in the land would congregate to dance in their palaces and estates. Our public ballrooms may not have attracted such illustrious patronage, for they were built for us common folk. But the ballrooms themselves were just as ornate and beautiful, and as grand in scale and size. They started popping up everywhere, and by the early twentieth century they had spread across the regions of the United Kingdom and were so popular that no good hotel worth its salt was without one.

Take a stroll down London's Park Lane and up through Piccadilly and you'll see what I mean. There's the Grosvenor House Hotel ballroom, there's one at the Dorchester, two more at the Ritz and the Savoy – all within a mile of one another, and that's just to name the cream of the crop. They were grand affairs, beautifully decorated, often with an Art Deco theme; they had sprung wooden dance floors, a stage for the band and sometimes tiers for seats and balconies. In the larger hotels they even had their own entrances.

People would flock to these ballrooms for dinner dances, not just on a Saturday night but midweek as well. They'd come to see the band play, they'd socialize and they'd dance. In the course of the evening they might also be treated to a demonstration dance given by a professional couple; these were immensely popular and a nice little earner if you'd made something of a name for yourself as a dancer. If you were doing well you might be giving five demonstrations a night. You'd start at one hotel, do a couple of dances, then hop in a cab to the next venue.

Not everyone could afford a night out at a top London hotel, of course, and so slightly more modest versions of those ballrooms were created round the country, until every city or large town had a ballroom or palais where people could come to meet, socialize and, above all, dance. At one point in the last century every major outlet of Burton, the menswear shop, had a ballroom above it – it was that popular.

The first major ballroom I danced at was a place called the Rivoli Ballroom in south-east London. It was the most wonderful place and I hadn't seen anything like it before in my life, having only ever danced in church halls up until that point. It was all decked out in red velvet, with rhinestones on the walls and chandeliers hanging from the ceilings. It felt as if it had been transported from another world and had mistakenly landed there in Brockley. (Back then Brockley was the kind of place where you'd have been worried about stopping at traffic lights for fear of getting your wheels nicked.)

There is always a sense of anticipation and excitement when you arrive at a ballroom for the first time knowing that you are going to take to its floor that night, especially when it's a really beautiful one. You test the feel of the floor, see where the band is going to be playing and where the audience will be, and once you get going that dance you spent so long rehearsing in the studio suddenly comes alive in the new surroundings and transforms into something quite other.

BLACK BOTTOM

A black bottom might be what you'll get if you fail to master the art of ballroom and keep falling over, though in this case Black Bottom isn't an injury but a dance. It hailed from the dance halls and clubs in America at the turn of the last century and with its jaunty moves and actions – bent knees, crouched torsos, pelvic manoeuvres – it was a hugely popular dance. Sadly, like so many of the wonderfully named dances of that era such as the Grizzly Bear, the Kangaroo Hop, the Turkey Trot and the Bunny Hop, the Black Bottom, which was the most popular of them all at the time, eventually fell out of fashion. It was replaced by a succession of new dance crazes that included the Charleston, a dance that was so fast and frantic that if you failed to master it you really were left with a black (and blue) derrière.

BLACKPOOL

'Blackpool, my Blackpool!' OK, so I realize it's not my Blackpool as, hailing from Kent and now being a Londoner, I am not a resident of that seaside town. Neither is that my line. I have stolen it from Kit Hallewell's book of the same name, which is a chronicle of the Blackpool Dance Festival over the years. However, I wholeheartedly agree with the sentiment.

Blackpool gets quite a lot of flack as a resort, which to my mind is quite undeserved, but anyone interested in dance loves this town because it's the capital of ballroom and is where all the major dance competitions, including the British and the World Championships, are held. More than the capital, Blackpool is the Mecca of ballroom dance.

Blackpool boasts not just one but two ballrooms. There is the Tower Ballroom, famous for its amazing architecture, its Wurlitzer and its sprung floor. And then there is the Empress Hall at the Winter Gardens, which is also home to the opera house. The Empress is a ballroom on a large scale – which is why the British Championships are held there – and it is quite magnificent to look at. But while the Tower might be smaller it's incredibly ornate, and its beautiful sprung floor is a joy to dance on. I can't help but get a thrill when I perform there, even after all these years. And I'd like to think that when I do I light up the town as much as the Illuminations and give as much Pleasure as its Beach. But I think that might just be wishful thinking on my part.

BOSSA NOVA

Bossa Nova was a popular style of music, a wonderful fusion of jazz and samba, which emerged from Brazil during the fifties. Just as night follows day, when we have a new music trend we need to find a dance to match it, hence the invention of this dance. The Bossa Nova never enjoyed the longevity of its other Latin cousins and was rarely taught in dance classes after the sixties, but it is still a lovely little number.

Bossa Nova translates as 'new wave' or 'new beat' and, while it comes from the family of Latin American dances that includes the Rumba, the Cha-cha-cha and the Salsa, it has a slightly softer character. This means that it involves more of a swaying to the rhythm of the music than dancing on a beat. So, with our body kept straight but our hips gently swaying, one arm resting on our stomach, the other outstretched, we move in time to the music, soaking up its sultry tones. Think João and Astrud Gilberto's rendition of 'The Girl From Ipanema'

– if you are tall and tanned and young and lovely and everyone you pass gives an admiring whistle, this really could be the dance for you. If you're like the rest of us mere mortals, do give it a try anyway because it's actually quite straightforward.

BOTAFOGO

A Botafogo is a dance step or variation in the Samba, although it can appear in other Latin dances, and it takes its name from a beachside area in Rio de Janeiro, where the Samba was born. Basically it's a classic three-step variation, and you can dance these steps forwards, backwards or to the side. The variation is usually repeated several times during the dance. Because of the tempo of the music it is usually danced quite quickly, so you need to be light-footed. If you have feet of concrete I wouldn't attempt it, but it's always great to watch.

There are several different variations of the Botafogo, including the travelling Botafogo, the shadow Botafogo and the criss-cross and contra Botafogo. A simple breakdown of the basic step is as follows, though. Start by facing the wall and then on the count of one, cross one foot across your body. Then transfer your weight slightly as you make a quarter turn. On the count of two replace the weight on the other foot and turn again so that on the count of three you have completed the figure. If you haven't muddled it, you should now be facing the centre of the dance floor. As a three-step pattern the footwork in a Botafogo is actually quite straightforward – what makes this variation difficult to master is the weight change as you move from foot to foot, and with that we want to add some rather ornate hip action to really get into the Latin spirit.

It's fast, it's furious and it's hot. And it also captures the essence of Brazil, so if you haven't got the carnival spirit or are a bit flat-footed, don't attempt a Botafogo ... you'll probably just end up Bota-fudging it.

C IS FOR ...

CHA-CHA-CHA

Ah, for the Cha-cha-cha, possibly one of my favourite Latin dances. Why? Because it's lively, it's rhythmic, it's energetic, it's danced to a quick tempo and it's hugely uplifting whether you're dancing it yourself or simply looking on.

The Cha-cha-cha came out of Cuba before the Second World War, and even its name is fun. 'Cha-cha-cha' is onomatopoeic – referring to the sound of the scraping of the güiro, the Latin American percussion instrument that would have accompanied the music, and also to the scuffling sound of the dancers' feet. And 'Cha-cha-cha' also refers to the three hip movements that make up the dance.

It has its origins in the Mambo, a dance that originated in Haiti, but by the time it had reached Cuba it had become a Triple Mambo – essentially a Rumba, but danced with extra beats. In the early fifties Pierre Lavelle, a leading dance teacher of his time, saw it performed in Havana and became such a fan that when he returned to Britain

39

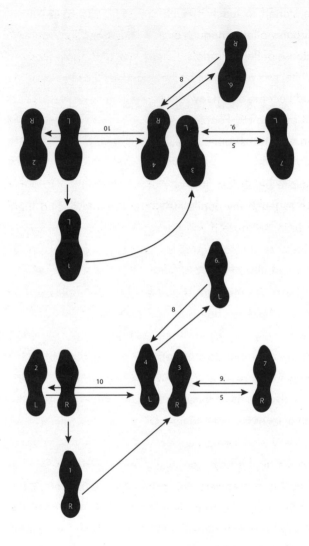

he started to teach it. With the 1953 recording of the Cuban violinist Enrique Jorrin's 'La Enganadora' and the release of Pérez Prado's 'Cherry Pink and Apple Blossom White' two years later, by the mid-fifties the Cha-cha-cha had become a firm favourite on dance floors all over the UK and the US. People loved it because it was fast, it was fun and it was rather flirty.

Despite being fast, it is one of the dances that I always like to teach my pupils first when I'm introducing them to Latin, because if you have good rhythm it is actually quite easy. It also showcases a melting pot of Latin styles and variations. Essentially it's all about abandon. The footwork is important, but it's as much about moving those shoulders and hips.

I always think girls do a great Cha-cha-cha. Now, boys, I'm sure you are great at it too but the girls just look fantastic when they do this dance: it's those fleet feet and fast spins with quick stops that they could do on a sixpence that make it so sexy. And then once they've stopped they're off again and it's all the boys can do to keep up with them. Ola Jordan is a complete firecracker when it comes to this dance. Her Cha-cha-cha is something to watch, it really is. (Mind you, like most men in this country I'm of the opinion that she's something to watch even if she's just standing still, with no offence to her husband and fellow dancer James!)

The Cha-cha-cha starts with the couple facing one another. Their bodies aren't touching but their hands are in a double handhold – holding hands, palms facing their partner. The man, who leads, stands with his weight on his right foot and his left 'free' leg out to the side; his partner mirrors this position. In the Cha-cha-cha the dance begins on the second beat, with a two-count, and on that the man will transfer his weight over to the left foot. On three, when he steps forward, the weight is transferred again to the original foot. On the fourth, he will step to the side onto his left foot again, once more transferring his weight. In the meantime his partner mirrors his every move. I've boiled it down to a very basic description, but in many ways it really is as easy at that. A really great Cha-cha-cha depends on four things: synchronicity, rhythm and maintaining a good hold, but above all on not finding yourself on the wrong foot. It's very hard to find your feet again once you have lost the step.

As long as the beat and tempo are correct you can dance the Cha-cha-cha to anything you want, even if it is really contemporary. But I feel that slightly takes away from the spirit of the dance, so I prefer to stick to Latin-style music. That's just me being an old stickler, though: what you really need is the speed. When you are just starting, go easy with the speed in the Cha-cha-cha, otherwise you'll find yourself on the floor with your legs in the air. But once you've got it down, as the kids say, double up the time and make it fast using a lot of steps.

These days the Cha-cha-cha is often interpreted as a happy, cheeky dance, which rather grates with me because it should anything but. It's a hot and steamy dance that oozes sex appeal. This was a dance performed by girls in the nightclubs of Cuba, dressed in tight pencil skirts, seamed stockings and high heels, and the music was sexy too; hot and earthy. It's all about the small, tight steps, the clicking of the heels and that subtle wiggle of the hips. Add to that what I call the 'Marilyn Monroe' move, where you kick your knee and ankle in, holding one arm to the chest as though you have just been caught in the shower and are trying to cover your modesty, and you're away.

CHARLESTON

Taking its name from the harbour town in South Carolina in the States, the Charleston was arguably the most popular dance craze ever to hit these shores. It was the early twenties, and having just emerged from the darkness of the First World War we were entering a new era, both culturally and socially. It was all about a time for change.

Social etiquette was becoming more relaxed, we saw the emergence of the Flapper girl and hemlines were rising – as Irving Berlin noted, 'a glimpse of stocking was rather shocking'. So when a new music trend called jazz started to be played over here we couldn't help but embrace it. The question was how to dance to it; with its lively and quick tempos this wasn't something to Minuet to. So, when word had it that there was a jaunty new dance style that befitted the music of the day we flooded in droves to our local dance halls to learn how to do it.

The Charleston, as we know it today, is characterized by a series of recognizable variations. It is all about the swivelling of the feet and the knees, the fast footwork, the kicking of the heels and the swinging of the arms back and forth. And – most memorably – the crossing the arms over the knees and the 'drying of the nails' hand action. These are the Charleston's signature moves. But what does it feel like to dance to? Well, it's fast, fast, fast! A good modern Charleston to my mind should be a comedic Charleston with lots of play-acting and role-playing, capturing the Vaudeville spirit and sense of musical comedy. A bad Charleston is one that doesn't swivel; it's just kicking and more kicking. If you do it that way you might be better off on the football pitch (and stand to make a shedload more money should you turn professional).

When the Charleston was first performed in the twenties it began with a simple twisting of the feet in a rhythmic yet quite understated way. It was an instant hit in America and it wasn't long before it was performed in Vaudeville acts across the United States. However, as with all dances, it evolved to keep pace with the music of the day; as jazz music progressed the dance became increasingly fervent. A fast-kicking forwards–backwards step was introduced – and the dance eventually incorporated tap, as well.

One really can't underestimate the impact that the Charleston had at that time – it was an absolute sensation. People were mad for this new style of dance to the point where it was getting rather out of hand. It really kicked off in dance halls, to such a degree that towards the end of the twenties the walls of ballrooms across the country were hung with signs that said 'PCQ' in large letters. This stood for 'Please Charleston Quietly', which I think sums up this dance craze quite perfectly.

CHASSÉ

The chassé is a dance step that features in different variants in all styles of dances – ballroom, ballet, line dancing and even ice dancing. It's a sliding step, whereby one foot displaces the other as if it chasing it – hence its name, which comes from the French *chasser* ('to chase'). In ballroom it's all about the closing and the opening, or the feet – slide, close, slide. There are many variations of the chassé in ballroom dance. We have a whisking variation, the scatter, turning and promenade chassé, a chassé roll (which sounds good enough to eat) and the tipple chassé. There is even one called the tipsy – which ideally should be attempted when sober, please. Why are there so many different types of chassé? Because it's a linking variation that takes you somewhere else. I like to think of it as a preposition – the 'and', 'if' or 'but' of a dance that takes you into the next 'sentence' of the sequence. So please mind your language: if you put your chassé in the wrong place you're not going to make much sense.

CHOREOGRAPHY

Learning to dance is rather like learning a language – the more words you pick up, the larger your vocabulary will be, and in turn your sentences will be better constructed. After a while, with any luck, you'll start making sense. And so it goes for dancing. Once you've mastered a body of steps the better you'll become, and from there you can start to construct well-developed routines to astound your family and friends, as well as yourself.

When constructing a dance there are a couple of things to bear in mind. First, you need to know your partner's limitations. It's all about not running before you can walk, so don't start throwing in complicated manoeuvres if you have yet to master the art of putting one foot in front of another. A simply constructed dance that is well executed is much easier on everyone's eye than a complex routine that looks like a car crash. Second, if you are dancing competitively and there are going to be other couples on the floor, you need to familiarize yourself with the floor plan and know what space is available. We don't want you thrashing around like the proverbial bull in the china shop. And third, you should have a knowledge of which step finishes on which foot so that you know which one you will be able to lead off on for the next: the dance has to keep moving.

Now, not all dances need to have a narrative. Obviously some, such as the Paso Doble with its story of the bull and matador, depend on an element of storytelling, but I often think that narrative is overrated. It's the dance, the steps and the movement of the couple that tell us what we need to know, and inserting some complicated plot into the routine can detract from the beauty of the dance.

That said, constructing a dance is rather like writing a

story in that it needs to have a beginning, a middle and an end. We're looking to create a vehicle for character and emotion. So when it comes to the Waltz, we need to feel the romance of the dance; in the Tango, pure passion; and in the Charleston there is room for slapstick. Try to make sure you have understood the message of the dance before you start work on your routines. We don't want to see a raunchy Quickstep, a bull in the Rumba or any sexy hip swivels in the Foxtrot, thank you very much.

I'm not a great fan of choreographing for myself any more, because I feel that I have done everything I can do and think of after all these years of dancing. I have a tendency to churn out a variation on a theme of something that I have already done. Instead I like to get inspiration from working with new and different people. That's when I can get really excited and put a new spin on things.

Everyone has a different approach to choreography, but my route into a dance is always the same – I start with the music. I choose a piece that I think will suit the dance and the dancer (or dancers) and I just go from there. I put the music on, listen to its nuts and bolts and then map it out from the beginning of the routine, because unless I know where I am starting I don't really know where I am going and certainly won't have a clue where I am ending! When it comes to choreography on television with people who don't dance for a living, it's all about knowing your partner's limitations and strengths, which can be slightly challenging to say the least. As far as touring with my professional dance partner, the wonderful Erin, goes, that's another matter entirely. Indeed, it could be said that some of the best steps I've ever made up are the ones she's told me she wants to do!

COMPETITIONS

Competitions in ballroom dance aren't quite the same as the ones that you might have seen on one of the television dance shows. For one thing, it is highly unlikely that your dance partner will happen to be a well-known celebrity and second, you and your partner are not the only couple dancing. There can be as many as twenty pairs dancing at the same time, depending on the size of the floor. And the competition doesn't just last for an hour and a half: it is staged over a couple of days until you reach the final heat.

Along with hundreds of other couples you enter the competition on a Thursday morning and then you dance your way through the heats. First, there is a qualifying round in which you'll be expected to perform two numbers. With any luck you'll dance your hearts out, impress the judges and be through to the next round. And so it goes from there, heat after heat until the judges have whittled down the competitors into the quarter- and semi-finalists, and eventually the six couples who will dance in the final.

Because of this, you and your partner really need to stand out on the floor. In the early stages of the heats there is quite a lot of tension as the dancers crash around one another out there on the floor, vying for the judges' attention. This is one of the reasons why there are so many rules and regulations in ballroom: there are so many couples dancing together and no one wants them crashing into one another or getting into any argy-bargy.

As the competition goes on, the times between each dance get shorter and it can all become rather exhausting. Even the fittest of dancers will be dead on their feet, but you have to keep going, despite the pressure. You need to keep your wits about you because at this level everyone in the competition is of a pretty high standard. What you need to continue to do is to stand out, to grab the attention of the judges, to impress them with that extra dash of skill and flourish that your fellow competitors lack – and if you carry that off, then with any luck it will be you who'll be lifting the trophy at the end.

CONTACT

'There are only two places where indiscriminate hugging is tolerated. The brothel and the ballroom,' M. A. Ham once observed. Ballroom dance is all about contact, and in this particular recreation you aren't just encouraged to get to grips with your partner – it's one of the rules! But gentlemen, please, do it nicely and with a little respect for your girl, otherwise you'll earn a name for yourself – and not a good one, either.

COSTUMES

Oh, how we love a ballroom costume – so much so that I know some people out there have taken up dancing simply for the outfits. All those sequins and swirls of silk for the girls, formal attire for the boys and those rather raunchy little numbers worn in the Latin dances – it's like a child being let loose in a dressing-up box.

Costumes are important in ballroom. First, because they give impact and that's we are aiming for when we are dancing. If you walked onto the floor to perform a Waltz dressed in your everyday clothes it just wouldn't be right. You need to feel the part and so does the audience, because dancing is all about taking them to another world.

Costumes also tell us something about the dance we are about to perform. When Erin and I are on tour and she walks onto the stage in a sassy short outfit, giving it some leg, the audience knows we are about to perform a Latin number. When she returns for the next dance in a beautiful, sparkling, twinkling evening dress made of layers of frothing silk they expect one of the classic ballroom dances. Whatever costume she wears, Erin looks a million dollars and there is always an audible gasp from the audience as she makes her entrance. I have to admit I find this a little annoying, because when we entered the stage together, I always assumed that gasp was for me as well. It wasn't until we entered separately that it dawned on me that this wasn't the case. I'm going to have to rethink my outfits.

It is very important to wear the right outfit for the dance. If Erin and I are dancing a number that involves a few swirls she'll want a dress that enhances that movement. You want people to look at you, whether you are dancing on stage, in a competition or even just for fun. It's all about creating a spectacle.

In ballroom dancing the boys wear formal attire. In Latin they will have a Latin-style costume, which these days tends to be quite tight. Personally, I prefer the ballroom costumes, as I know I look better in a suit than in a shirt slashed to the navel. There is more to a tail coat than meets the eye, though, so I'm afraid you can't just don one you've found in the back of your grandfather's wardrobe. It must be specially tailored to allow you to move. The armholes of the coat where the sleeves are attached are cut to allow the male dancer to lift his arms up freely. (In a normal jacket the armholes are much tighter, and if you performed that action repeatedly you would hear a terrible ripping sound.) The coat is also designed not to ride up when you are using your arms or lifting your shoulders.

The dresses for the girls need to allow for movement as well, and it's important to make sure that the cut of the frock is right for the style of the dance. In ballroom the girls always wear long evening dresses, but in Latin anything goes, and these days they tend to be really quite skimpy (especially on television, though that might have more to do with the dads watching). But while those outfits might seem as though they are made of very little, they are actually very carefully constructed, with a lot of flesh-coloured netting and mesh to preserve the dancer's modesty at all times. In the rules of competition dancing outfits can't be too revealing, and often there will be a dress monitor to make sure no one is looking too overexposed – some people get all the best jobs! I might be applying for that position when I retire.

Back in the old days on the competitive circuit it would probably be your mother who was given the task of running up your costume, but now it is all a little more serious and everyone seems to have started turning to professional costumiers, even at amateur level. These dress designers are highly skilled and it's better to invest in a couple of costumes that really suit and fit you, rather than leaving it to your mother – who probably also has better things to do than sew sequins onto spandex through the night.

I love a good costume, especially if it's channelling a little Fred Astaire. I even quite like some of the Latin ones if they're not too revealing, and if I'm honest about it I even like a little bit of Lycra. Like most dancers I've also suffered a few 'wardrobe malfunctions' in my time, and had the odd zip go just before I'm due on stage. Usually these can be fixed in time – though bear in mind that it's probably best not to use safety pins when you're wearing a catsuit.

CUCARACHA

The Cucaracha is a variation in the Cha-cha-cha. A Cucaracha – which rather unfortunately is the Spanish for 'cockroach' – is a sideways step. You step and close, and step and close. It's as simple as that, except that it also involves a hip swivel. The hips go one way, and the steps go the other, as you transfer your weight from one foot to another. Beginners often find it hard to get their hip movements right, but this swivel is important, because if you leave it out it just looks as if you're shuffling from foot to foot in the queue for the bathroom, which is not quite the sexy look required in Latin.

D is for ...

DANCE CARDS

Ballroom dancing is not a solo activity; if we are going to dance the night away then we need to find a succession of partners to take to the floor with. Easier said than done, some might argue, because for us lads summoning up the courage to ask a girl to dance can be a heart-stopping moment. Will she say yes, or laugh in my face in front of the whole of the dance floor? And if she does agree, how do I know that the tempo of the dance about to be played is going to be right for her? I don't want to insult her sensibilities when they start playing a Cha-cha-cha if all I'd intended was to do a nice little Rumba with her ... As for the ladies, well no one likes to be seen as a wallflower. We all need a dancing partner if we are going to go to the ball.

Towards the end of the eighteenth century a solution to this age-old problem was found in the form of the dance card. At the start of the dance gentlemen would put in their request to dance with a lady, and this would be lodged in a small booklet, usually worn on her wrist. They first became popular in the society balls of Vienna, but by the beginning of the nineteenth century the fashion for dance cards (or *programmes du bal*, or *Tanzkarte*, to give you the French and German equivalents) swept Europe, and later America. They became increasingly ornate and decorative over time and at very plush events would not only have space for the names of the girl's dancing partners but often a list of the actual dances, the composers of the tunes and sometimes even a menu card – they would later serve as a souvenir of the evening.

Eventually dance cards fell out of style here in Europe,

though they remained popular on the other side of the pond until the end of the twenties. And they made their mark on common parlance – hence the expression 'pencil me in', which we still use today.

DANCE CLASS

Dance has always been an important social activity, and we all want to be able to do it well and not look as though we have two left feet, even if we do. Before anyone ever dreamt of social networking, dance was one of the ways in which we interacted with one another: whether it was to place ourselves within society, make contacts and friends or find a potential mate. So learning to dance well wasn't just some self-indulgent pastime, it was an important social skill.

In the early days, when people wanted to learn the latest dance trends, those who had money would call upon their dance master to teach them how to do it. This all started in the courts of Vienna, Paris and London, where dance skill was considered an imperative. As time went on and the dance fashions kept changing, us common folk also wanted to keep up with the dances du jour and so we started taking lessons as well. In Britain in the nineteenth and early twentieth centuries attending dance classes was an important part of any well-to-do girl's education – especially if she was about to be presented at court as a debutante. She would spend many hours a day practising under the tutelage of her dance master or mistress. It was all about knowing how to present herself in polite society, so the tutor didn't just teach steps and moves but also covered how to walk into a room, how to sit, how to hold herself and how to curtsey. These tutors were the arbiters of social etiquette and would verse their pupils in the parlance of physical good manners. Nice girls – and boys – danced nicely: that was the form, and so as soon as you could walk you would be sent off for your weekly dance class with Madame Volcano, who would put you through your paces.

Not everyone could afford these private sessions, of course, but that didn't mean that they didn't want to learn how to dance well too, which explains the emergence of communal dance classes – and dance schools. These became increasingly popular at the turn of the last century when they started to spring up around the country. As the ballroom dances started to become standardized, everyone was desperate to keep up with new techniques and they took it all very seriously. This, of course, was wonderful for the professional dancers of the day as they were able to cash in on their reputations by opening their own dance schools, which invariably took their name.

These schools thrived for the greater part of the last century, but entered a decline in the seventies. A new style of dancing, one that wasn't in partner, took hold: disco. As disco fever erupted, no one wanted to know how to waltz or rumba any more, and the classes started to empty. Oddly, it was with the release of one of the great disco movies, *Saturday Night Fever*, that the dance schools found a solution: suddenly everyone wanted to learn to dance Travolta-style. Cannily the schools started to teach disco classes, the halls began to fill up once more and – excuse the pun – found a way of staying alive.

When I first started to take dance lessons it wasn't at some posh London class under the tutelage of someone with a French name, and we certainly didn't do etiquette. Instead I went to a local class in my hometown in Kent. It was conducted in a church hall by a mother-and-daughter team – Beryl and Velda. They spent the entire class puffing away on cigarettes as they taught us the Foxtrot on a Wednesday afternoon, but I can't help but think fondly of them because they did introduce me to dance.

★ ★ ★

DANCING SHOES

Girls, I know you love your shoes, especially your heels. And it baffles me that you insist on having so many when us lads can happily make do with just a couple of pairs, but when you take up ballroom dancing I'm afraid you're going to have to leave those six-inch stilettos in the wardrobe and invest in a proper pair of dancing shoes. Your dancing shoes can have a heel, but not a high one. Otherwise you are not going to be able to move well and you'll be in danger of skewering your partner's foot with the spike of your stiletto if you make a mistake.

Dancing shoes should have a good sole, shouldn't be too stiff — sometimes suede is a better option than leather — should feel comfortable, and above all should stay on your feet; so no slingbacks and certainly no flip flops! All this might sound obvious, but you should see some of the footwear worn by my pupils when they first turn up to class. A good pair of shoes will give you stability and make it easier for you to use your feet.

DOUBLE LOCK

Double locking is always a good thing to do when leaving the house, but in ballroom dance terms it refers to a manoeuvre. It is similar to a chassé, but in this variation you cross behind (as opposed to in front) and tie it in to whatever step you have just performed.

DYNAMIC

The term 'dynamic' in ballroom refers to the energy between a couple when they dance. It's the speed of the movement, the velocity of the jumps, spins and turns, the shape of the motion, the spring of the step and the pushing and pulling of two bodies as they move together. It's about the physicality of the dance and what the couple are doing to one another as they move. The easy way to tell the difference between a good dynamic and a bad one is that if it's bad, there just won't be any. It's as simple as that. If it's good, the couple will have it and you'll see it. Oh, and if the dynamic is working you'll get quite sweaty as well, which secretly I quite like!

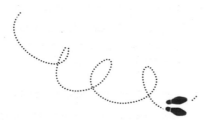

ENTRANCE

We love a big entrance in dance. Why? Because it creates drama, sets the mood, is theatrical and gives immediate impact. I'm a great believer in entrances, so much so that I often find myself making them throughout my day, even when I am entering my kitchen to make some coffee ... and I'm alone.

When you are dancing on stage or performing a demonstration dance, your entrance is key. You want to present yourself in character to your audience – even if that audience is just your Mum and Dad in their living room – and give an indication as to where this dance is going. You need people to sit up and take notice and have a sense of anticipation. And frankly, if they haven't realized that you're there in the first place, there is really no point in carrying on with the routine. You'd be better off catching the next bus home.

Now, in ballroom competitions making a grand entrance isn't easy, because you are already on the floor, standing with your partner in hold. If you're lucky the compère might announce your presence – 'Ladies and Gentlemen, please welcome to the floor … ' – but that's as good as it gets. Yet even if you and your partner are just standing there in position, you can still make an entrance of sorts. In those first few seconds, simply through eye contact or the way you stand in hold you can create mood, atmosphere and drama, and once the music begins those first few steps can set the tone of the ensuing dance.

It's all about finding interesting ways to begin a dance, and I'm not going to pretend that it's easy. It's rather like writing a novel and finding the perfectly compelling opening sentence. So while your entire dance might go through multiple incarnations during rehearsal, with any luck by the time you get to the floor to showcase it you will have produced a memorable opening.

In exhibition dances or on television shows you can really have fun with your entrances and make more of a statement, whether you enter the floor using one of the staircases, performing a cartwheel or doing a double backflip. You can also rely on a prop or two for real impact. This is especially useful if your partner isn't very good on their feet, when you can use this device to detract from their footwork.

EXHIBITION DANCES

In competition dancing there are strict rules and regulations as to what you can do when performing a dance, but in exhibition dancing anything goes. You don't have to break the rules, because there are no rules, and you can do anything you want – mix your dances if you please, add steps and variations to a dance that otherwise shouldn't be there, put in some flips, kicks and swings … and above all, you can lift your partner into the air. So if you are quite showy by nature (or bored of your partner and want to hurl them out of sight) then you might be better suited to exhibition dancing than competitive ballroom.

EXIT

Just as your entrance to a dance shouldn't be insipid, when it comes to the exit you need to make it big. We want to go out with a bang, no matter what we're dancing. Over the course of the dance we have tried to build momentum stage by stage and keep building it right to the end. So that last step we take needs to have a sense of finality about it. No going out with a whimper! Whether we find ourselves clasped round one another at the end of a Latin number, performing a running finish in a Quickstep or ending a Waltz with a beautiful flourish, we need to add a full stop to that final sentence. So don't go waffling endlessly on; leave that to the judges.

EYE CONTACT

For those of you who are a little shifty and find it hard to look someone in the eye, I would suggest that you stick to the ballroom dances rather than the Latin ones. In ballroom we don't look one another in the eye as our connection is all in the hold, while the Latin dances are all about eye contact. So if you are in any way optically challenged, I'd suggest a trip to the optician before you attempt any of the Latin routines.

And when considering eye contact, you need just the right amount. You don't want to be staring each other down as though you are about to have a punch-up. You also need to adapt it for the style of the dance. For the Tango it should be intense and full of fire and passion, for the Salsa you're aiming for a connection that is full of fun and fizz and slightly saucy, and for the Rumba you should be exchanging sensual glances. Note: this does not mean leering – even if you are partnering me.

F IS FOR ...

FAN

I'm not referring to my thousands of adoring admirers here (in other words, my mum) but to a variation that occurs in both the Rumba and the Cha-cha-cha. The lady starts in a closed position, opens up into a sideways one, and then into an open position like a fan. She can use her arms in a variety of positions as she performs the variation – up or down to make it more flamboyant. If you do try it, you need to keep it graceful, otherwise you'll knock your partner out. No matter what you feel about him, if you want to give him a smack in the nose, save it until you are off the dance floor.

FEATHER STEP

The feather step is the first variation in the Foxtrot. It's comprised of either three or four steps, depending on what version you are executing. The three-step variation is forward, forward, forward for the man and back, back, back for the lady and you simply add another step if you are doing a four-step. I know, girls, it always seems to be the case that you are going backwards. As someone once observed: 'If God had intended us to do ballroom dancing he would have made women's knees bend the other way.' But if you are in the hands of a good man then he should lightly but expertly steer you around the room. If you're in the hands of a bad one – escape!

There are two reasons why we call this step the feather: first because the foot curls like a feather. And second because on step three the man is stepping outside of his partner with his right foot, outside of the track that she is on. This makes it look like they are 'feathering' – as in carpentry when you are building a nice fence or shed. The pattern of footsteps resembles those overlays of wood. I realize that comparing a ballroom technique to one used in woodwork might seem a little incongruous but it's one that works for me ... and you should never underestimate a shed. Like many men, I've had some of my best moments in one.

FLECKLE/FLECKERL

One of the questions I'm most frequently asked about ballroom these days is what a fleckle is. This is partly because my dear friend and long established dance professional Len Goodman, seems to be obsessed by them when he talks about them on television.

A fleckle – or, more correctly, fleckerl – is a variation in the Viennese Waltz. Fleckerl is the German word for a 'small step', and that's what we have here: a small step, danced in rotation. The dancers come out into the centre of the dance floor and dance on the spot. Unlike other steps in which they may move forward, here they rotate round and round one another. The steps should be small, neat and nimble so they appear to be seamless, and it should be danced quickly so that the couple appears to be spinning on the spot. The great skill of the fleckerl lies in staying in the same place. Move off that spot and you've had it.

There are two types of fleckerl – the natural and the reverse fleckerl – depending on whether you are turning clockwise or anticlockwise. It's a hard step to master properly and not one I would recommend to a novice, but when danced well it is magic to behold. A well-executed fleckerl can make a dance, and to master it is to master the Viennese Waltz.

Although it's a signature step of the Viennese Waltz, the fleckerl actually originates from a drinking game that was practised in the Bierkeller of Austria hundreds of years ago. Two men, fuelled by alcohol and the encouragement of the other patrons, would jump onto a small table and whizz round each other, running around in circles but retaining eye contact until they became completely dizzy and fell off. The last man standing was the winner of a draught of beer. It might seem like a long way from a drunken lad's night out in Austria to the vision of an elegant couple gliding round the dance floor, but it's a great image to keep in mind as you try to make your fleckerls flawless.

So when people ask what it is that Len Goodman loves so much about the fleckerl, the honest answer is that I haven't got a clue – only that he's an East End boy and he loves a good drinking game. But that's only a suspicion and I'm sure he would refute that!

FLICKS AND KICKS

Flicks and kicks in a dance routine shouldn't be used to torment your partner, no matter how much they're annoying you; instead they're an embellishment or an adornment to a dance. In a Tango we use them to lure our partner in an alluring, coquettish way and in the Jive, which is full of them, they are performed in sync with the beat to enhance the upbeat spirit of the music.

FLOORS

They say that the perfect dance floor is a sprung maple one because it gives the best surface to dance on; you can move and glide across the floor with ease and it feels comfortable underfoot. As far as I'm concerned the springiness of the floor is neither here nor there, although I really wouldn't recommend trying to dance on concrete because that's a bit hard on the old knees and shins. Wood's the thing – you can dance on other surfaces, but they're never as good.

So, we want our floor to be made of wood and we also want it to be clean. No sticky surfaces, thank you very much; if you've spilt your drink on it get mopping before you attempt your Foxtrot, otherwise you're going to be dancing on the spot. Some years ago there was a big ballroom competition. By the final it was all getting very tense – so much so that the existing champions were getting rather hot under the collar about losing their crown that night. One might have assumed that they would up their game in some way but, no, they had other plans, and surreptitiously threw handfuls of sand on the dance floor to make their competitors unsteady on their feet. It could have been murder on the dance floor, but fortunately they were rumbled. Shocking, I know – I would never dream of sabotaging or otherwise causing havoc on a dance floor!

OK, so that's not entirely true ... Once, in my youth, I was competing at the Albert Hall in London, in the International Championships. Despite it being one of the most beautiful and illustrious venues to dance at and this being the International Championships and all that, I'm afraid to say that we really did seem to be dancing on stone, for rather than laying a nice wooden dance floor for the event, the organizers had simply painted the existing floor a shade of red to make it look a little more glitzy. It was a nightmare. The floor was so 'sticky', as we say when referring to a floor with no give, that you couldn't glide or slide or gain even a little bit of lift. You couldn't twist your foot, turn it, pick it and up and then place it ... and there was no question of being able to execute any rise and fall. As a result, none of us knew how we were going to make it through the competition.

Fortunately, we were offered a solution to the problem when a chap who had formerly worked in the car industry suggested that it might be a good idea if us competitors used a little silicone spray on the soles of our shoes. I wasn't entirely convinced that this would work, but I was willing to give anything a go. And after a quick spray of my dancing shoes I was gliding and sliding across the floor.

With our feet now functioning, things were going well in

the competition, and Erin and I had passed through all the heats and were heading towards the final rounds. Victory beckoned, or so it seemed, had it not been for a rather irritating couple who, sensing the competition, decided to get tactical and took it upon themselves to bash into anyone they saw as a threat – targeting poor Erin time and time again. I was so riled by this I took matters into my own hands. During a break between rounds, in which the dancers often take their shoes and their jackets off while waiting to perform again, I found my rival's shoes and the can of silicone spray and gave him what he deserved – an extra two layers of the stuff just for good measure.

Suffice to say he never made the finals. In fact he had a particularly bad next round, which culminated in him sliding into the front row through his whisk and chassé and pulling a hamstring in the process. It wasn't cricket, I grant you – it was ballroom dance. And as far as I am concerned, no one messes with my Erin.

FOOTPRINTS

Nowadays if we want to learn the latest dance craze then we are just a click or a flick away from it, but back in the days before we had television, music videos or the

Internet, keeping up with the latest dance trends wasn't so easy. Of course, as I mentioned before, you could always take classes from a dance instructor, but not everyone had the time or the money for that. It was a chap called Arthur Murray who solved this problem, with the invention of the 'footprint' dance diagrams.

Born in 1895, Murray was a draftsman and also a dance instructor, who in the course of his long career taught the likes of the Duke of Windsor, Eleanor Roosevelt, the Woolworth heiress Barbara Hutton and the cosmetics queen Elizabeth Arden how to step in time. Murray had learnt his technique from Irene and Vernon Castle, the husband-and-wife dancing team who did much to popularize ballroom dance, and he was much in demand both as an instructor and for his demonstrations across America. It was following one of these exhibitions and during a chance conversation with the American politician William Jennings Bryan that Murray first hit upon his idea to bring dance to the masses. According to legend, Bryan had told him: 'Just teach them the left foot and don't tell them what to do with the right until they pay up.' It was a casual quip but it got Murray thinking, and in time he devised his dance diagrams, which he began to sell via mail order. These sheets of drawings showing footprints of the dance steps could be placed on the floor, and so in the privacy and comfort of your own home you could learn the latest dance trend simply by following the pattern. It was a simple idea but a successful one: within a year, half a million of his courses were sold. Murray, who married his dance partner Kathryn Kohnfelder, later went on to open a hugely successful global chain of eponymous dance schools.

FOXTROT

The first thing you need to know about the Foxtrot is that it's the most difficult of all the ballroom dances to master. You need good posture, and above all you need to be able to walk in a straight line, so it might be a good idea to abandon that second glass of wine — just for the moment, at least. It might be a difficult dance but it's a magical one. It is quiet, beautiful and very emotional, and whether you are watching or performing it you should feel at the end that you have been swept away by the sheer romance of it.

The Foxtrot is all about walking. Sounds straightforward, but as with all these things it's not. It's all too easy to find yourselves stomping round the dance floor like a pair of elephants. You are going to be using an opening stride step, but it needs to be smooth, elegant and seamless: what you are trying to achieve here is a long, flowing

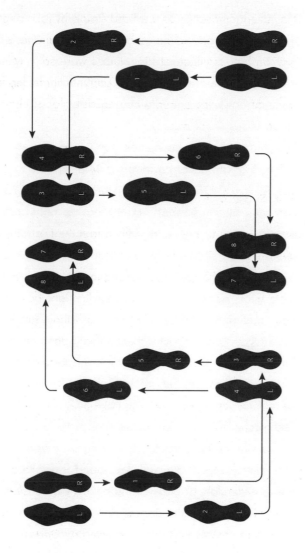

movement across the dance floor. You and your partner need to be in perfect harmony and in time; that's the glue that holds this dance together. If you can nail that, it will be marvellous; if you don't you'll finish all knotted up and frankly, it's going to be a disaster.

The character of this dance lies in its linear direction and its passing foot action, and this is what gives it its flow. The key is to roll your body weight through your feet. Body contact is also important – right breast to right breast – but you need to be slightly offset from one another to avoid a nasty collision. On top of this there is the issue of the music. The Foxtrot is danced to a 4/4 rhythm, four even beats per bar, but – and here's the rub – in the basic pattern of the dance there are only three steps. This means you have to make three steps somehow fit into four beats. This is why we use a slow-quick-quick rhythm, and that's what puts the 'trot' in Foxtrot.

Technically, you can dance the Foxtrot to any piece of music with the right tempo, but being an old-fashioned boy I always like to dance or see it performed to one of the all-time classic songs of the era to evoke the style, aura and magic of the dance. So I like to return to the jaunty hits of Cole Porter or Irving Berlin.

Now, if someone in the ballroom dance world starts

talking to you about the Trots, please don't assume that they have a condition necessitating regular trips to the bathroom. Trots were a style of walking dance hugely popular back in the day. At the beginning of the last century we had a veritable repertoire of them. There was the one-step Trot, the two and then the three (logical when you think about it), as well as an array of dances that take their names from the animal kingdom: the Turkey Trot, the Bear Trot, the Possum Trot and the Lobster Trot. You didn't have to don an animal costume to dance any of these. What you needed was to be nimble on your feet, so much so that the 'walk' became a dance.

All these dances fell out of fashion and faced extinction following the birth of the Foxtrot. But how did the fox get into the trot? Well, ladies and gentlemen, let me introduce you to Mr Harry Fox, circus performer, professional baseball player and star of the American Vaudeville circuit. He first performed on the music hall stages of San Francisco before moving his act to New York, where he would dance on the roof of a converted *jardin de la danse* with the Dolly Sisters.

There are many conflicting stories about how the Foxtrot evolved, so for this I am going to refer to Josephine Bradley's version of the tale. Bradley was the great pioneer of the dance and, along with her partner G. K. Anderson won the first Foxtrot competition ever to be held in twenties London, so she should be the authority on this one.

According to Bradley's account, a new rhythm of music had just come into fashion, and with it came a dance style to match. As with all these new crazes it was first showcased at the Vaudeville theatres, and one night there was to be a demonstration of this latest fad by a couple of professional dancers. At the last minute the leading man was suddenly taken ill and was unable to perform. But the show must go on, as we say in show business, and Harry Fox was asked to step into the breach.

Now, though Harry could dance, he wasn't acquainted with this routine. But he was a game old boy and rose to the occasion. Rather than stalling he simply and instinctively followed the rhythm of the music. At first he began with a simple Trot, but as the tempo of the music quickened he did too, concerned with keeping up with the beat and not boring the audience with a pedestrian routine. He had nothing to worry about: as he quickened his pace and added more steps, dancing fervently round the stage, the audience lapped it up and cheered him on. By the end of the routine he had brought the house down. And that, boys and girls, is apparently how the Foxtrot got its name.

It wasn't long before this new style of trotting caught on. People loved the speed of it and went wild when the bandleaders played the ragtime and jazz tunes that so suited this dance. In the States it was Irene and Vernon Castle, the spectacular husband-and-wife dancing team, who brought the Foxtrot to the fore, while in the UK it was Josephine Bradley and Frank Ford who did much to popularize it. Not long after their first Foxtrot win, the dance was standardized. Of course, as time went on and the music got even faster, suddenly the Foxtrot didn't feel quite so exhilarating or pacy and it was eventually superseded by an even more spirited version of the dance – the Quickstep. But fortunately the Foxtrot stood the test of time and came back into fashion again when dancers realized that it was far too exhausting to quickstep all night and that they needed a little reprieve.

It might be a difficult dance to perfect and it demands practice, perseverance and bucket loads of patience, but if you can master the Foxtrot then you'll be able to waltz through any of the other dances on the ballroom menu.

G IS FOR ...

GAPPING

Mind the gap here, because ladies and gentlemen, the key to ballroom dancing is all about body-to-body contact. We need to see you in hold, giving the impression that you are dancing as one. That said, we don't want to see you super-glued together from head to toe so that you can't move properly – we need to have a little space between you. Depending on the dance you are performing you might experience high contact, lower contact, slight contact or hard contact, but there is no dance in which we want to see any large wind tunnels between you. So no gapping, please. If in any way you are repulsed by your partner then try Latin – either that or trade them in fast.

H IS FOR ...

HANDS

One of the questions people often ask me is why the judges of television dance shows seem so obsessed with the contestants' hands, when surely it's the feet they should be concentrating on. The lovely choreographer and dance guru Arlene Phillips has been known to shudder visibly at the sight of misplaced or badly held hands. As for director and choreographer Craig Revel Horwood – show him a pair of mitts that aren't pointy enough and he'll shoot you a look to say that he really isn't amused.

To give them their dues, they have a point. Of course, feet – and footwork – are key to dance, but hands are important too. A perfect dance can be ruined by poor use of your arms and hands. I don't want you to look like an octopus falling out of a tree, nor like you've got two fists of ham resting on your partner's body. And as for thumbs, put them away – we're not trying to hail a cab here, we're ballroom dancing. But before you start to fret, good handwork is relatively simple. There aren't lots of complicated rules or positions for hands. All you have to remember that hands are the continuation of a line. They should be held out all the way down to the fingertips because arms don't end at the wrists. They should be soft but not floppy and should have a sense of purpose. They can be used in a gesture of giving or receiving.

Think of your hands as decoratively punctuating the lines of your body. The message should come through your body and out through your hands. Boys, listen here: at no point should your hands cause your lady to misunderstand your intentions. And girls, don't grip the man to death. We don't want to see finger marks when we take our jackets off! I want to feel the love, not the pain.

HOLD

You might have heard the term 'closed hold', but what is it and how do you do it? Let me explain, before you and your partner start striking poses that might cause a few raised eyebrows and blushes among the judges. Yes, you can touch each other – but only to a point, and the degree to which you do it depends on the style of dance.

A simple breakdown of hold is as follows. Start by standing facing one another with your feet slightly apart.

Boys, I want you now to raise your left arm so that your hand is slightly above the level of your shoulder. Your elbow should be a little bent. Now place your right hand lightly just below or on your partner's left shoulder blade, picking up your elbow so it matches the height of your left. Don't whatever you do lift your shoulders because you'll look stiff and awkward, you'll restrict your movement and your neck will disappear down your tail coat. I need you standing tall and looking elegant at all times. It makes for a better line and gives the impression that you know what you're doing, even if you haven't got a clue.

Girls, you need to raise your right arm and place that hand in the man's left, palm to palm. Again, you need to make sure that your right elbow is slightly bent. Now place your left hand on the man's upper right arm just below his shoulder. You should be standing in front of each other but slightly offset, with your right fronts facing each other. This will prevent you from crashing into one another and allow you to move. In Latin the hold is the same but your bodies won't touching, as you'll be a foot apart from one another.

The reason that the lady dances to the right of the man goes back to the days when men all went about wearing swords, even when they were dancing. Because the majority of people are right-handed, it was the convention for a man to wear his sword and scabbard on the left-hand of his belt so his weapon could be drawn quickly and easily. To avoid a nasty accident, or the lady tripping over the sword, she would need to be to his right when he put his arm round her back. So it is true: real gentlemen – and ballroom dancers – do dress to the left.

HOLLYWOOD

We've travelled to South America to learn our Latin, we've twirled round the ballrooms of Europe to perfect our ballroom ... but if you really want to know about dance then I want you to come with me to Hollywood. Never mind about the air fare, we're just going to make a quick pit stop at our local DVD store, settle down on the sofa with a nice cup of tea and watch one of the old-time silver screen classics, which are not only hugely entertaining but serve as a blueprint for everything you need to know about dance.

I'm taking you back to the forties and fifties when the genre of musical film was at its height. We're watching Fred and Ginger in *Top Hat* and *Shall We Dance?*, loving Gene Kelly in *Singin' in the Rain* and *An American in Paris* and we might even go a little further back in time to admire the work of the great Busby Berkeley, the director and musical choreographer responsible for all those spectacular, complex and kaleidoscopic dance routines featuring legions of chorus girls. We're watching *Easter Parade* with Judy Garland, Rita Hayworth in *Cover Girl*, *The Bandwagon* and that wonderful Astaire and Kelly routine 'The Babbitt and the Bromide' in Ziegfeld Follies and – one of my personal favourites as it combines two great passions in life, dance and golf – the golf ball routine in the Fred and Ginger classic *Carefree*.

Throughout the forties and fifties musical film was all the rage and the public couldn't get enough of this type of movie; in retrospect, who could blame them? They were hugely entertaining, had a feel-good factor, were spectacular to watch, featured great music that stays with us today and they also showcased some of greatest talent of the time – performers who could not only sing and act but really knew how to dance as well – Astaire and Rogers, Frank Sinatra, Esther Williams, Anne Miller, Cyd Charisse, Sammy Davis Jr, Lucille Ball … the list could go on and on.

My friends probably would have had a pop at me at the time, when I should have been getting into *Star Wars*, but as a young lad these classics had a huge impact on me. I was entranced by them and would often try to copy their routines. Even today I draw on them when I am planning a dance. So it's not strictly ballroom dance, as mainly they are dancing the American Smooth style, but I can't help but feel inspired by them. Towards the end of the fifties musical films fell out of fashion, but in recent years we have seen a revival thanks to the popularity of movies such as *Strictly Ballroom*, *Chicago*, *Saturday Night Fever* and *Dirty Dancing*, which I have to admit is a film I have never seen, though I do know enough about it to know that 'no one puts Baby in the corner'.

IMPERIAL SOCIETY OF TEACHERS OF DANCING

ISTD refers to the Imperial Society of Teachers of Dancing (and not some embarrassing condition you might have contracted on the dance floor while performing the Argentine Tango). The ISTD is the leading organization when it comes to the teaching of ballroom dance. Based in London and established in 1904, it is an educational faculty that sets the syllabus for dance education, providing courses for dance teachers and training in dance styles for students. It also acts as an examination board for those training to become certified teachers. They're an important bunch of people, so I'd better not say any more as I need to stay on the right side of them. But one thing's for sure, you don't need treatment for it.

INJURIES

Ballroom dancing might look graceful and elegant, but please remember that this is a contact sport – dancers can easily suffer as many injuries as footballers or rugby players. Pulled hamstrings and broken ankles are a frequent complaint, as are foot and leg strains, bunions, blisters and rashes. The ballroom dancer is prone to back problems, hip displacement and the occasional groin injury too, which isn't very pleasant.

To date I've been very lucky when it comes to injuries. I once suffered from burning balls, but that's probably more to do with the fact that I put a tube of Deep Heat in the wrong pocket than having incurred a disco wound or worn too much Lycra.

So, ballroomers, please try to dance as nicely and tidily as possible to avoid these complaints. I want you on the ballroom floor, not in traction.

INTERNATIONAL STANDARD

When you're watching a ballroom dancing competition on television you'll often see the judges getting in a right pickle about which steps should or shouldn't have been included in a routine. Now, between you and me, some of them can be a little pedantic and tricksy about such things (of course I'm not talking about you Len, God forbid!). And I'm sure that you at home are wondering what they are on about and why it is all so important. Well, let me explain. The answer to this lies with what is known as the International Standard, which is basically a list of ballroom and Latin dances that have been regulated by the World Dance Council. These standards were first developed in England and are now adhered to across the globe, and woe betide anyone who strays too far from the specified steps and techniques. Think that's all a bit petty? Well, to put it into context, without the International Standard ballroom dancing would be like playing a sport with no rules. We all need to know what we are – or rather should be – doing when we dance, otherwise it's just freestyle. And us dancers might have our John McEnroe strops when we get pulled up by the judges, but they do know their stuff (especially you, Bruno Tonioli – and you can send the cheque to the usual address).

Call me a bit of a teacher's pet here, but I'm all for that, and even though I admit that sometimes I have broken the odd rule or two I do think the art of ballroom should remain as pure as it can. I don't like it when people start to muck around with it. So, ladies and gentlemen, don't over-egg the pudding otherwise it's just not going to taste or look very nice when it's served up.

J IS FOR ...

JITTERBUG

The Jitterbug is a swing dance and a derivation of the Jive and, like its sister the Lindy Hop, was born in America during the Second World War. It takes its name from twentieth-century slang for those suffering from alcoholism who had the 'jitters', because when you watch this dance at first glance, it seems as if no one on the dance floor is following any kind of set routine – instead dancing with wild, carefree abandon, going crazy and looking quite out of control. Think fifties movie: the guy with the leather jacket and the slicked back hair, the girl in the great big skirt with her ankle socks and ponytail.

There are kicks and flicks, leaps, jumps and throws in all of these dances, and to be honest the layperson might find it hard to differentiate between the three styles. But a basic rule of thumb is that the Lindy Hop features high kicks and big leaps, the Jitterbug is a bit more open and swivelly, while the Jive is much more about swinging. (When I say that I am not talking a car-keys-in-the-bowl moment, but about how you move to the music.)

JIVE

The Jitterbug, the Lindy Hop and the Jive were popular dances of their era, but only the latter stood the test of time, eventually becoming a standardized ballroom dance. It was first introduced to these shores from the US, by the American GIs stationed here during the Second World War, and it wasn't long before this style of frenzied dancing caught on. Against a backdrop of war, with couples not knowing whether they would ever see one another again, this fast, frisky, energizing dance gave a few minutes of reprieve; a chance to forget their troubles. It's a dance where anything goes – it's about freedom of expression, swinging round one another, throwing your legs around and letting go, having fun and enjoying the lively, upbeat tempo of the music.

I think everybody loves the Jive, and I know the contestants on dance shows look forward to it because it's fun. But a really good Jive is hard to nail. One of the celebrity dancers who I think has truly done it justice is the actress Jill Halfpenny. Her performance is so good and convincing that, frankly, she could enter a proper competition against amateurs or even professionals and still do well. She's technically brilliant and of such a high standard that she leaves many of us pros with gaping jaws, wondering whether we should be reaching for our P45s.

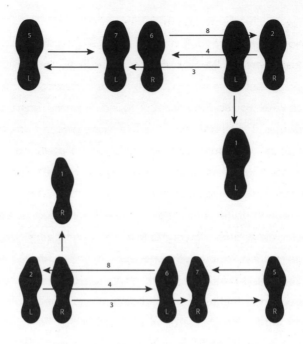

Jive may have come to Britain in the forties, but the origins of the dance go much further back than that. The jury is out as to where it first originated, but towards the end of the nineteenth century it started to be danced across the southern states of America; by the 1880s it was danced competitively. There were no glitter ball trophies to be had back then – instead the prize was more modest, usually taking the form of a cake. Given how much energy had been expended on the dance floor this was arguably a little more useful, and it is the reason why the Jive was also known as the Cake Walk.

The Jive evolved, and during the early twentieth century the music got faster and the dance became the latest craze to hit the ballrooms. And it has since weathered all the new music trends, up to and through the rock 'n' roll years, until it became the newest of the Latin dances to be standardized. In the old days the Jive was all about swinging in time with your partner, but in time variations were added to it – kicks and spins – which gave it a different kind of energy. It's now all about being on your toes, swinging and bouncing at the same time and dancing off the accent of the music, particularly on the second and fourth beats of the bar.

As the Jive evolved it caused its share of controversy on the dance floor. Some objected to the fact that it could be danced alone, as you don't have to stay in contact all the time, while others believed that it had a 'corrupting influence' and tried to force it underground.

The Jive never went away though, and it is still hugely popular today. Only recently I went to a Jive club over in Kennington and was looking forward to spending the evening dancing away and, well, showing off a little. It soon became apparent, however, that my interpretation of the dance wasn't quite the same as the regulars on the floor, for in ballroom the Jive is a very choreographed and precise number, while theirs was much more fifties rock 'n' roll freestyle. I got some rather curious looks as I did my thing.

But that's the beauty of the Jive – it's so recognizable and distinctive that it is the one dance that we all think we can do, no matter our age or ability. It's the dance that gets your Uncle Clive up off his feet at the family wedding as soon as the band starts playing some rock 'n' roll, dragging your aunt onto the floor with the line 'Come on love, let's show these youngsters how to jive properly.' Yes, she might end up staggering off the floor with a dislocated shoulder, and he might collapse head-first into a plate of pavlova, having taken that final swing a little too far – but at least they had a good time while they were dancing it.

JUDGING

So what do you look for when judging a dance? On the positive side, what you want to see is style, musicality, fluid movement, harmony, timing, poise and good footwork. What you don't want to witness is a couple that are out of time, with bad posture and no communication between one another.

Judging in competitive dance is very different from the judging we see on the television dance shows. For one thing we don't use paddles with scores of one to ten: that's what they do in ice dance. Instead, competition judging is done by a series of ticks in the early stages, and you are not being marked down but up. If you score the requisite points then you're through; if not, it's back home for you. When you reach the final they start using points and the final six are placed. The other difference is that the judges aren't sitting at a desk but are instead dotted round the perimeter of the floor, marking you as you dance past them.

An expert eye can judge a good dance a glance but it's really what the judges don't see that counts. If you are dancing well, it should all be seamless and 'invisible'; it's the mistakes that stand out. In my opinion, what you need to be a good judge are two things. First, experience: I really don't think you can start saying what a good Cha-cha-cha is unless you have attempted one yourself. I'm not saying you need to be the greatest dancer in the world, but you should at least have taken to the floor in your time. Second, you need a track record, because knowing what high-quality dancing is is not about reading up on it in a book. You should not only have danced a bit but you should have taught people – it's just not enough to look at the dance as a whole and then come up with the line that the couple 'made it their own'.

I've judged in competitions over the years and I have to admit it is not a task that I particularly enjoy because of the weight of responsibility that goes with it. Having been on the other side, as a contestant, I know how much the judges' decisions can affect you and your partner. It's like playing God.

Naturally, I have the utmost respect for judges and hold them in high esteem, but I often think the best judges of dance are the paying public who come to watch it; they're the ones who have just dropped a fiver at the door to watch you perform, so their opinion really counts for something. Having said that, I hasten to add that the four *Strictly* judges are without exception wonderful, brilliant human beings, each with a fantastic eye and unerring taste. And yes, I do mean that sincerely …

★ ★ ★

K IS FOR...

KELLY, GENE

If any of you men out there think dancing is for sissies, then I want you to take a look at the life and career of one of the finest dancers ever – Hollywood star Gene Kelly, an award-winning American actor, dancer, singer, film director, producer and choreographer. Born in 1912 and raised in Pittsburgh, Pennsylvania, as a young boy Kelly was enrolled at a dance class by his mother, along with his elder brother James. The two brothers were teased mercilessly by the other children in their neighbourhood, to the extent that there were fisticuffs in the street when the boys returned home from their lessons, and both eventually dropped out. It wasn't until Kelly was 15 that he danced again. And when he did, his primary motivation, apparently, was that he thought it would be a good way to meet girls. I had the same idea ...

Kelly was a both a gifted sportsman and a talented student, but his family didn't have a lot of money and so he realized that if he was going to go to college he would need to earn some cash. He started entering local dance competitions with the hope of winning the prize money. That he did, time and time again, and it wasn't long before he started moonlighting outside college as a dance instructor. This sideline proved to be so lucrative that Kelly and his family decided to set up a dance school of their own.

Although he was academically inclined, Kelly tired of college and dropped out of law school, deciding that he wanted to make a career for himself as a dancer and entertainer. After a spell in New York where he tried to gain work as a choreographer, Broadway beckoned. After a series of hits, which included Roger and Hart's *Pal Joey*, it wasn't long before Hollywood came calling. He was signed to the studios and the film work kept pouring in. He went on to work with Judy Garland, Cole Porter and Lucille Ball in those first few years. But the film that would propel him to stardom and secure his place in the Hollywood firmament as both an actor and a dancer was *Cover Girl* with Rita Hayworth, in which Kelly performed a stunning, and now famous, routine with his own reflection.

Throughout the forties and fifties, when musical films were at their height of popularity, Kelly was one of Hollywood's most bankable stars, and he went on to make hit after hit. Today he is probably best remembered for what I consider to be two of the all-time greats in this genre – *An American in Paris* and, of course, *Singin' in the Rain*.

What made Kelly exceptional as a dancer was that he was able to bring athleticism and energy to dance, while at the same time incorporating modern ballet into his routines, which was completely innovative for the time. Yet despite doing so he never once looked like a 'sissy'. He was the ultimate leading man. Some would say that was because of his looks, for unlike Astaire he was macho in his build, which would lead him to quip that when he donned tails like Fred he still looked 'like a truck driver'. But perhaps that was what made him such an inspiration. He made dance accessible to everyone – especially men. And, as he once said: 'Any man who looks like a sissy while dancing is just a lousy dancer.'

L IS FOR ...

LATIN DANCE

It might be dead as a language, but as a form of dance it couldn't be in better health. I'm pleased to say that Latin dance is alive and kicking and very very popular. It's a style of dance that we all love to perform, because like the continent it hails from, it has so much to offer: romance, tradition, sensuality, rhythm, spice and heat. There are so many wonderful dances that have come out of Latin America over the centuries, from the Salsa to the Merengue, the Mambo to the Bossa Nova, and they are all so much fun to dance, especially if you're in the mood for a party. But not all of them could make the grade as standardized dances and so to date we have six: the Rumba, the Paso Doble, the Cha-cha-cha, the Jive, the Tango and the Samba.

The Latin dances performed in ballroom are far more choreographed versions of anything that you would see danced in the nightclubs or dance halls or even on the streets of Latin America, but they retain the essence and spirit of the original dance forms. And while each of the dances is completely different when it comes to style, tempo, mood, emotion and signature moves and steps, the same rules apply to all the Latin dances. There must be good eye contact, the dancers should move together and there is great interaction between the partners even though they are not touching. Usually there is much more of a story than there is in ballroom. And on top of all this you also get to be a little freer with your clothing. So if you fancy slipping into a skimpy little number for a swivel or two, or want to give your chest hair a little airing, you might find that Latin is for you.

LEADING

In ballroom, the man does all the leading. That might not be very progressive in this day and age, ladies, but that's just the way it goes I'm afraid. He's the boss, he's the decision maker – but it's only for three or so minutes and once you're off the floor the roles can be reversed. And you know what, girls – once you've accepted that and got into the dance you might find you actually quite enjoy it!

Someone once said to me that a good man follows what he leads and, boys, I want you to remember that at all times. You might be in charge of the dance but I don't want that to go to your head. You mustn't forget about the needs of your partner. She's not a dog on a leash, nor should she be steered round the room like an object. We need to adopt a little chivalry here. You lead, she follows, you let her do her thing and then you come back to her and lead again. It's all about consideration and some good old-fashioned manners.

So if I have a girl in hold I take her to the place she needs to be and throughout I'm timing her and she's timing me. She does her little thing and I don't move until I feel that she has finished and then I'm ready for her again. Think of it as akin to driving your girlfriend to the shops, letting her have the time to try on a frock or two without impatiently huffing or puffing as you check your watch, but instead looking interested and engaged at all times. And then once she's made her purchase, driving her home again obligingly. OK, so maybe by using that analogy I have made leading sound harder than it actually is …

A good leader does the following: he never leaves his woman in a position where she is unsure of what to do next, he never takes her off balance and he never gets out of time with her. If you throw her off balance it's not right and it's not fair because it's your duty to make her look and feel good. If you come in too soon to do your thing, then you're not just interrupting her when she's talking but, frankly lads, you're just showing off. And dancing, as I keep saying time and time again, is about partnership and harmony.

But girls, know your place! He's in charge, whether you like it or not – but remember he's only doing it for you, to make you shine. Beside every great woman on the dance floor there is a great man.

LIFTS

You've seen them performed in the television dance shows, in the theatre and in films, but let's get something absolutely clear here: in competitive ballroom dance lifts of any kind are illegal. I realize this might come as something of a disappointment, as you fantasize about recreating that moment from *Dirty Dancing* when Patrick Swayze has Jennifer Grey perched horizontally on two fingers in the lake, but in ballroom it is banned and if you try one in a competition you'll get short shrift from the judges.

Why aren't lifts allowed? Well, as with all the fun things that are ruled out of our lives, it all comes down to health and safety. As I've described, in a competition dance you might have up to twenty couples dancing on the floor at the same time. If they all start lifting their partners in the air it's going to get terribly messy, and we want them to enjoy the dancing, rather than spending the night en masse in A & E.

So, in ballroom the rules dictate that you must have one foot on the ground at all times. You can lift your partner from there a little and allow for some height – so long as her foot is still making contact with the floor. We don't allow for plate twirlers in ballroom.

That said, I have to admit that I do love a lift or two, whether I am performing one on stage or watching one during an exhibition dance. You have a strong man and a rather bendy girl, and he's holding her in the air with one arm, spinning her round, then he drops her down and the crowds gasp, only for him to suddenly sweep her up in his arms at the last moment as the crowds cheer. It's pure theatre – but it's strictly not ballroom.

LINE

When we talk about having good line we are referring to a mixture of posture and poise. It's the way that you present your body to your partner in order for her to want to dance with you, and vice versa. You want to come together with perfect body lines that match and fit together, and you want to give your partner something to dance against. Without a good body line you are aren't going to have good balance, by which I don't mean the ability to stand on one foot for a prolonged period, but rather the balance of motion and partnership.

LINE OF DANCE

'Line of dance' refers to the direction that you are travelling in around the floor. You are in hold, the music has started and you're walking – but 'Which way?' I hear you yelp. Well, the first thing to remember is that in ballroom we only ever move anticlockwise round the room, especially when we are performing the progressive dances, which include all of the ballroom dances and also the Paso Doble and the Samba. It's essential never to go against the line of dance – remember, there will be other couples on the floor and if you go the wrong way you'll become the most unpopular people in the room. If we all started going any which way we wanted, there would be the most almighty crash. It's like driving the wrong way up a one-way street – it's illegal, going against what I like to think of as the Highway Code of ballroom. If you do see a couple about to collide with you, you need to have your wits about you. Boys, this means doing a quick manoeuvre out of their way. And girls, if your partner isn't aware of the oncoming traffic, give him a signal.

Now you're moving round the floor anticlockwise, there are a few other things to bear in mind. You can go into the centre of the floor and out again, but never back on yourself (maybe a step or two at most). There's an imaginary line down the centre of the room, helpfully called the Centre Line, and we never, ever cross it – otherwise terrible things can happen. We can dance round the Centre Line at the outside of the room, dance towards it and then out again to the wall, but we don't cross that line. It's rather like the offside rule in football, and almost as complicated to explain, but again the reason for it is that in competitive dance you aren't the only ones on the floor. To go into the centre or cross it would upset the flow of the other dancers. The other thing to note is that in a competition the judges stand around the ballroom floor marking you, so they need to be able to see you.

Some of the Latin dances such as the Cha-cha-cha and the Jive are far more stationary, so you are slightly less restricted, but when it comes to the big numbers you still have to bear all of this in mind. And one more thing: you must never, ever stop and talk on the dance floor, no matter how pressing you consider it to be. So if you feel the need for a natter or an angry word, take yourselves off the floor to the side of the room and out of everyone else's way.

MAMBO

Although it involves complicated footwork, there is a sense of freedom about the Mambo; it's so enjoyable to dance, as you can really let your hair down. That is if you've still got any left.

The Mambo is a great number that first started to be danced in the thirties in Havana. The craze for Mambo later spread further afield than Cuba, though, and became fashionable in America and Mexico in the forties and fifties, thanks largely to the Cuban bandleader Pérez

Prado, who composed a litany of popular songs for this style of dance.

What does the Mambo look like? Well, to the untrained eye it's pretty much like the Salsa, really, in that it's fun, lively and full of swivelly hip work. And like the Salsa it is danced to an upbeat Latin number, imagining that you are creating some heat at a wonderful little dive in downtown Havana after a Cuba Libre or two. But, ballroomers take note, though the Salsa and Mambo may look similar at a glance they are danced to a different beat. The Mambo is danced on the 2/2 count, the Salsa on the 4/4. Bear this in mind when you try to impress your Latin lover with your moves, because otherwise you are going to end up looking like you've been fast-forwarded.

MIRRORING

Mirroring occurs in most of the Latin dances. We stand in front of our partner and mimic (or mirror) what they are doing and the movements they're making – rather as we might do when we have been in a relationship for too long.

* * *

MUSIC

It's all very well getting to grips with your footwork, but you also need to verse yourself in music, because when you are planning your routine you need to choose a piece of music with the correct tempo and mood to accompany it. You can't be dancing the Tango to a slow, melodic tune – you want strong staccato rhythms to match the drama of the dance. And when dancing a slow number full of romance and emotion you certainly don't want any bump and grind.

'Tempo' refers to the speed, or the number of bars per minute, of a piece of music. In ballroom dancing we have what is called a strict tempo: the speed of the tune must remain consistent throughout the routine, otherwise it's going get rather messy and complicated. We also have what is known as 'time signature', which denotes how many beats per bar there are in a piece of music. When we talk about dancing in 3/4 time, as we do in the Waltz, what we are saying is that there are three beats to each bar. If it was a piece in 4/4, that means – you've guessed it – that there are four beats to the bar. (You don't have to be Einstein to work that one out.)

4/4 time occurs in dances such as the Cha-cha-cha, the Rumba, the Foxtrot or the Quickstep. But just because a piece of music has a 4/4 tempo, don't make the assumption that you can dance all of these dances to the same piece of music. For instance, you can't dance the Foxtrot to the same tune as the Quickstep because that's performed at almost double the speed. Similarly the English Waltz only has around 32 bars per minute whereas the Viennese Waltz has around 52. So you really do need to think about this when selecting your song. And remember too that in terms of beat, ballroom is danced on the first beat while Latin begins on the second.

When we refer to the rhythm we aren't just talking about whether you and your partner are dancing in time to the music (although that is quite important) but also the accentuated and recurring beats and the lengths of the individual notes, which is what gives a dance colour, emotion and spirit. Try to bear all this in mind, especially if you are planning your wedding dance, because there is nothing more incongruous as the bride and groom taking to the floor for the first time to perform a romantic Waltz, only for us all to discover that 'their song' happens to be an up-tempo, loud and shouty hip hop number.

When you have been dancing as long as I have, one of the challenges is trying to make each routine you put together look different from the last. So whether I'm touring or competing I try to keep things fresh when it comes to selecting music to dance to and mix it up a little. I'm a bit of a sucker for the old tunes, because they work with the ballroom dances and I'm an old-fashioned boy at heart. But that doesn't mean I'm not open to performing those kinds of routines to more contemporary music either.

What I listen for in a piece of music is how it builds, because that's how I can start envisaging where the dance might go – let's take Cole Porter's 'Night and Day' as an example. As I'm driving along in the car listening to it, I can see how my partner and I will perform it. Or you can take a great track like Abba's 'Dancing Queen', and already you have a great narrative to play with in terms of the lyrics alone.

N IS FOR ...

NATURAL TURNS

A natural turn is so called because you are turning to the right. If you were turning to the left you'd be performing a reverse turning variation. You begin by facing diagonally to the wall and end diagonally to the centre. The expression doesn't mean that you are a natural when it comes to turning.

NEW YORK

New York: a city so great they named it twice. But we aren't talking about that great city when we refer to the 'New York' in ballroom but rather to a variation that occurs in the Cha-cha-cha and the Rumba. It's a step-through in the Promenade Position and can be danced to the left or right. Like the city, it's quite showy and rather glam, so bear that in mind when you attempt it.

O IS FOR ...

OPENING OUT

Opening out sounds like something you might do in psychotherapy, but it's actually just the reverse of the New York. I think this is a little unfair really, as they could have given it a slightly more interesting name to match its sister – the LA or the Washington, perhaps.

OUTSIDE PARTNER

This is not a command you give your partner when you want to take your fight outside, it's a move in which the man steps to the outside of his lady's foot and feathers her.

OUTSIDE SWIVEL

And as with the outside partner, the outside swivel does exactly what it says on the tin – you swivel outside of your partner. It can be used in most dances, but you see it most in the Tango. You swivel outside of your partner and begin to turn on the spot and that's it! If you are asked to do an outside swivel it doesn't mean you have to go into the street or your back garden to perform it.

P IS FOR ...

PARTNER

They say it takes two to tango and they're not wrong there. It also takes two to foxtrot, quickstep, rumba or to perform any one of the dances that fall under the umbrella of ballroom dancing. The difficult question is how to find that perfect dancing companion.

Just as when you go in search of 'the one', there are certain things to look for before you enter a ballroom marriage. You need to find someone you get on with because, with any luck, you are going to be spending the rest of your dancing life with them. You should try to find someone with a nice temperament, even if it is different from yours, because you don't want to be at odds with and shin-kicking each other at the end of every evening. And you should share a sense of humour because, as with any relationship, there are going to be ups and downs. Most important of all, you should also try to make sure that you are physically compatible.

Now this is where you have to be really careful because, shallow as it might sound, height and weight are very important when you are selecting your dancing companion. If you are a very slight man there is no point in trying to dance with a girl who is a former Olympic swimmer (even if she did win gold), simply due to the fact that she's likely to be quite broad in the shoulder and the balance of your frames will be out of kilter. Not only will you not be able to move well together but, I hate to say it, she's just going to look big, which isn't very fair on her. So my advice is to pick on someone your own size, or a lady who is slightly smaller than you, and leave our swimmer to a more macho companion. Likewise, if you are a rather petite girl, don't set your sights on the tall, hunky fella, no matter how much you like him away from the floor, because when you are on it the partnership isn't going to gel. Ballroom dance is all about the hold and Latin about the eye contact and if you're physically mismatched you're going to be seriously disadvantaged.

A good partnership is all about shape and balance. Many moons ago, before I turned professional, I had the opportunity of partnering a girl from Germany. She was extremely lovely, very easy on the eye and a great dancer, but the problem for me was that she had quite a big ribcage. I don't mean that rudely – it was just that for my size, frame and arm span it was never going to work well. She needed someone taller and stronger, and so we went our separate ways, parting amicably – it being a case of 'it's not you, it's me'.

In the course of my career I have danced with many partners on both the amateur and professional circuits. In my capacity as a professional on televison I've partnered a list of celebrities, all of whom have been terrific fun to work with and a complete surprise to me. Although I have got used to being presented with a challenge now and again! It's not always about the ability to dance – things like differences in your respective height can be a real challenge. But, in the words of one of my partners, if nothing else you can try and be memorable and have a good time together, which brings me to my next point about finding the perfect partner – you need to have chemistry.

You don't need to be in love with your partner, but when you are out there on the floor the audience needs to feel that you are, whether you are dancing the Rumba or the Waltz. There needs to be a spark between you in a Cha-cha-cha, you should feel the temperature rising during a Tango and you must capture the sense of harmony that should exude from the Foxtrot. So if you haven't got that chemistry between you and it's all a bit flat, it's not going to work no matter how technically proficient you are.

The perfect partnership isn't about two individuals both being very good, either; it's about how two people work as a pair. I've seen people who are good individually but don't work as a partnership and in turn watched couples where one is far more skilful and yet somehow it just works. There was one World Champion who was a brilliant dancer but his partner wasn't up to his level. She was a nice enough dancer but she would never have been considered among the top ten great female dancers of the time. And yet they were unbeatable, winning competition after competition. Eventually they went their separate ways and he traded up. He found himself a new girl to dance with who was far more skilful. Everyone assumed this was going to be a match made in heaven but it wasn't, and he never won another championship again, which was a lesson to us all. If you find your ideal dancing partner, stick to him or her like glue. I've had the good fortune to dance with Erin now for sixteen years and I hope it stays that way and that she doesn't think of trading up, because over the years the more we've danced together the better it has got. What I love about Erin — aside from the fact that she is the most exquisite dancer — is that there is a steely determination about her. When we first met she had come over to England from New Zealand because she was determined to up her game as a dancer, and I realized then that anyone who was prepared to make that move and travel to the other side of the world, leaving family and friends behind, was passionate about ballroom. I really admired her for that. And she's also incredibly patient — she puts up with me on a near daily basis.

Not all professional dancers are quite as monogamous when it comes to partnerships. Take the case of Timothy Palmer. Born in 1907, Timmy Palmer was an exquisite dancer and a master of swing. He won the British Professional Championships in Blackpool not just once but three times, and with three different ladies. His first win came in 1932 when he partnered Miss Kathleen Price, his second was the following year with Miss Edna Deane and his third was in 1939 — he was in hold that time with Miss Ella Spowart. In the six-year gap between his second and third wins Timothy Palmer didn't compete at the championships. That wasn't because he'd lost his flair for dance, far from it. The reason he didn't make it to Blackpool was because he was serving time at Her Majesty's pleasure: when our Timmy wasn't dancing he was a bit of a 'tea leaf' and had been sent down for the offence of holding stolen goods. Once released he made a victorious return to Blackpool and to date he remains the only person to have won the championships with three different partners – so maybe a little ballroom promiscuity can pay off.

PASO DOBLE

The Paso Doble is the most narrative of all the standardized Latin dances, telling the complete story of a bullfight. It's a dramatic dance, one full of passion and intensity, and to dance it well you need to be both focused and convincing, otherwise it's all going to look rather silly.

In this dance the man takes the role of the matador, or *torero* as they say in Spanish. He is strong and dominant, entering the dance floor as he would the bullring – with a sense of bravado. He is about to take on the mighty bull, and he looks death in the eye. But ladies, fret not, you are not the bull in this dance so you can step out of that pantomime cow outfit and change in to a beautiful swirling frock instead. You play the part of the matador's cape or *cappa*. So you are acting as his shield – you are strong yet fluid, always feminine and instinctively responding to your matador's instructions so that you work in perfect harmony. You are matching both his shapes and positions in order to lure, toy and tease the bull towards and away from him and then gracefully moving, twisting, arching or turning away from the beast at the last second, until at the end of the dance the game is over and there is the final moment of death – the coup de grâce.

Now, I love to play the role of the matador. I like to think that's because my mother is Spanish and so it's in my blood, though I am sure there are some who might think it's because I'm prone to talking quite a lot of bull at times. But the real reason I enjoy it is because of the drama, excitement and the intensity of the dance and the way the story unfolds scene by scene. There is a strong Spanish feel to this dance. The flair of the movement, those beautiful flamenco steps, even the name Paso Doble (which means 'two steps'), all hail from that wonderful land.

The dance itself is characterized by a series of variations such as the Chasse Cape, the Coup du Pique, which is a decoration with the cape, and the Sixteen, whereby you take eight steps with your partner, perform a little

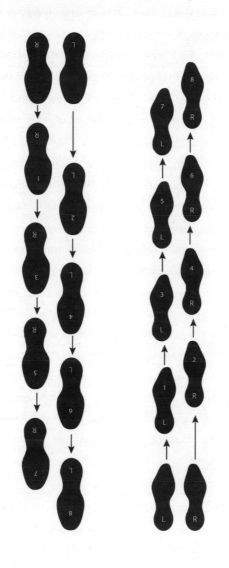

appel (or turn) and then another eight steps in another direction. Sounds simple enough – especially if you can count – but the Sixteen is an integral variation in the Paso as it gives strong marching feel to the dance. This manoeuvre is symbolic of the action the matador makes with his cape as he moves it round his waist, inviting the bull to charge. He steps forwards and swishes the cape as the bull charges past him, while all the time standing still. You need good shaping in this dance, which means an exaggerated movement where you lean to the left or right with your arms curved over the head, allowing for the imaginary bull to whizz past you. Your posture should be strong and toned from the tip of your toes to your fingertips, because matadors don't slouch.

If you get it right, this is a powerful, stamping yet elegant spectacle full of drama and intensity.

The Paso Doble was hugely popular during the twenties, right up to the start of the Second World War, both here and in Continental Europe. Monsieur Pierre, the professional dancer and exponent of Latin American dancing, mastered the art of the Paso with his partner Doris Lavelle, and when they gave demonstrations in London and Paris people would flock to see them. The Paso isn't danced socially here anymore, and features only in competitions and exhibitions, which is probably down to the complicated choreography of the narrative.

But if you do want to try it at home, please take note – you don't need a cape because one of you is the cape. It makes me wince when in television dance competitions or demonstrations the matador walks on stage with a glittery piece of fabric hanging from his hand or round his shoulders. Put it away, I want to shout. You have your cape and she's standing there in front of you! Now you're just Johnny Twocapes and it's turning into a circus act. Boys, you are the matador; girls, you are the cape. Another cape is just going to confuse the situation – especially if it's silver and covered in sequins … that really is a load of bull!

PICTURE STEP

The picture step is a rather like a decorative punctuation mark, a little line that you make having performed a couple of variations down the floor. It could be small throw of the arms or a sway. You look at it and think how lovely, because it's so pretty. But it actually serves as an important tool. This is because in dance you should never stop moving or break the line of the routine; the picture step allows for a feeling of continuity as you move on to the next part of your routine.

POISE AND POSTURE

A good ballroom dancer should always have poise. This will not only add to the look of each dance, but on a more basic and practical level will also help with balance. Poise in this sense refers to carriage and composure, but if we are going to split hairs it also refers to some basic dance rules. So ladies, for you poise means a slight curve to your left, with your head turned slightly so that you can look over your wrist to see where you are going and also where you have been. Your head is held high in such a way that it continues the line of your spine – rather than looking as if it has been glued to your partner's shoulder. As for you, boys, you should be standing with your weight slightly on the balls of your feet, which will give you enough propulsion to lead in ballroom. When it comes to Latin, both boys' and girls' bodies should lean slightly forward.

You also need to have good posture. 'What's the difference between poise and posture?' I hear you grumble, slouched on your sofa. They are pretty similar, I grant you, but the way I like to describe it is that posture is the nuts and bolts of good poise. If you stand well, then you will have good poise. Posture is all about making sure you are well aligned – that your hips are over your ankles, your shoulders are over your hips and your spine is going in the right direction. It's a bit like house and home, really. House is the concrete version of home; posture is your house, poise is your home.

As far as I am concerned, posture is one of the most important elements of ballroom dancing. The better the posture, the better the dancing, because of the proximity of the couple. I don't want to see any hunched or stooped backs. Quasimodos are in danger of kicking each other to death. Having the correct posture is going to help you with your balance, movement with one another and also with weight transfer.

When I am teaching I always ask people to get into the correct dance position before we begin a class so we can perfect their posture, asking them to first lift their arms up and straighten their backs – but at the same time being mindful not to raise their shoulders too high, otherwise they'll look like a zombie. You boys should make sure that you are standing tall with your feet together and your head, shoulders and chest lined up over the centre of your feet. I want your arms to be hanging by your side and your ribcage lifted up, like a slightly puffed-up, proud bird. By adopting this stance you will at once look elegant and refined, no matter how uncouth you are in real life. And the girls will love you for it, as they always like a man who stands tall.

Ladies, I want you to do the same thing. I realize that this might make some of you feel a little self-conscious but I can't tell you the difference this will make to the line of your body, even if you are a little shy. By picking up your ribcage you'll release your hips, giving you much more freedom of movement – plus you'll look more graceful, taller and thinner! Who needs plastic surgery and diets when they have ballroom?

PROPS

Props are never used in competitive dance, but they often are in exhibition dance and it's quite fun to add a bowler hat or two into a Charleston routine, or a chair or street lamp into a romantic number. They are also quite useful if your partner isn't very footsure; they can keep the judges' and audience's eyes elsewhere. I've used a lot of props in my time, and for the most part they have worked well to enhance the routine. But one dance partner and I did once fall foul of a feather boa. The offending item managed to slip from her shoulders within moments of the dance beginning, fell to the floor and tangled itself round my feet as I stepped forward. Thankfully, I somehow managed to prise myself away from this snake of feathers and kicked it away but the dance was lost for us. So, from that moment on there were to be no more boas and I told her that if she really wanted one I'd get her a boa constrictor instead.

PRIZES

To borrow a catchphrase from my good friend Bruce Forsyth – dancer, star of the stage, film and television, singer, brilliant golfer, knight of the realm and much loved presenter: 'What do points make? Prizes!' And we all love a prize, no matter how big or small. Whether it's a purse full of cash, a shiny trophy to place on the mantelpiece or simply a cake (as was given in the first Jive competitions), it's nice to have something to show for your win.

That's certainly what ballroom dancer Sonny Binick thought when he entered a championship in Germany. Sonny was one of the great dance stars of the fifties and along with his partner Sally Brock he won the British Professional Championships a staggering five times. He was a favourite on the international circuit too, so it made sense to compete in the German championships, not least when the prize for the finalists was – drum roll – a black and white television! Now, I realize that you youngsters out there with all your smartphones, iPads, laptops, Blu-ray players and games consoles might think it strange that anyone should get so excited about the possibility of winning a telly. Let alone travel all the way to Germany to do so … But, boys and girls, in those days people didn't have a television set in every room of the house – in fact, most people probably wouldn't have had one at all, and would have had to rely on their more affluent neighbours if they wanted to watch something. Winning a TV back then was a really big deal, so when Sonny and Sally danced their way to first place they were over the moon.

Though the Second World War had been over for some years at that point, let's just say that relations between the British and the Germans were still rather tense. The hosts weren't too pleased that the Brits had won the competition, and when Sonny and Sally went up to the collect their dues from the prize table, rather than being presented with the television, one of the organizers picked up a canteen of dinnerware, which was meant for the runners-up, and handed it to them instead. Sonny was having none of that, though, and he pushed the man out of the way and grabbed the television set from the table, much to the amazement of the organizers and audience.

Nowadays, you don't tend to win a telly – it would hardly be worth putting your dancing shoes on for that. Instead you are more likely to win a cash prize. But these aren't exactly enough to send you into early retirement; we're talking about £10,000 at most in a larger competition, and that usually ends up going towards your costs. What we really win when we walk off with a trophy is prestige. This (especially if you are a professional) is what is going to raise your profile and status on the teaching circuit, which is where the real money is made. It's all about the glory of being declared the best and lifting that trophy or glitter ball above your head (although I have yet to find out what that feels like).

PROFESSIONAL

Some of us do things in life for pure pleasure, others do it for money – and that's the basic difference between an amateur dancer and a professional, like myself. I do it for the joy of dance – and the cash!

When we talk about amateurs in ballroom – or in sport – we don't mean that they are necessarily lacking in skill or should be seen as beginners. I know plenty of amateurs who are much better dancers than some of the professionals. It is just that they have yet to take that leap into the professional world, and qualify. So the amateurs would be working at another job by day and dancing by night, whereas the pros are dancing all day, whether they are giving lessons, taking lessons or practising.

However, both the amateurs and the professionals follow the same circuits, because in competitive dance there are categories for both. There was a time (before they changed the rules) when it was stipulated that you couldn't have two professions – in other words, you couldn't be a professional dancer and a bank manager or a doctor at the same time. As a result there were many truly gifted dancers who were forced to remain on the amateur circuit because they wouldn't give up their jobs and their tidy salaries. The transition from being an amateur to turning professional is arduous and involves a lot of practice, lessons and examinations, so you have to be very dedicated. I've been dancing since the age of fourteen and yet I only turned pro fifteen years ago. I know what you're thinking – 'that didn't take very long' – but I digress.

People often ask me what it is like to be a professional dancer. After all, it's not your average job. They want to know how I cope with the gruelling routine of all those rehearsals, the classes and the competitions that I used to take part in. And I admit that it's tough – dressing up in fabulous finery, sweeping a beautiful girl off her feet night after night – but someone's got to do it.

Q IS FOR ...

QUICKSTEP

Dancing the Quickstep is rather like falling in love for the first time. It will sweep you off your feet, take your breath away and leave you feeling elated and slightly giddy. This is one of the most exhilarating of all dances, one full of speed and splendour, and one of my personal favourites.

The Quickstep is a dance full of big swishing movements, to which intricate footwork is added – a smorgasbord of jumps, hops, tricks and, of course, quick steps. So you really need to be on your toes for this one. You also need to keep a cool head, for although it may look like a dance of abandonment, to achieve that effect you must have control. If it's danced well you and your partner should be flying into the air as you sweep across the room, running, jumping, skipping and spinning to a fast tune.

The Quickstep was born of the Foxtrot – her rather excitable son and heir. It came from the music halls of the New York suburbs in the twenties, when people were starting to get a taste for music with faster tempos. The big bands, who were largely responsible for dictating the latest dance crazes as they introduced new music trends, were now playing jazz and ragtime, and somehow the Waltz, the Tango and the Foxtrot were no longer cutting the mustard on the dance floor. And so during this time a new form of Foxtrot was devised – a quick-time Foxtrot, with the original dance sped up, sometimes to as fast as 50 bars per minute. New steps and manoeuvres were also added. At first this new dance had Charleston moves in it – hence its name, the 'Quicktime Foxtrot and Charleston' – but by the later twenties the knee movement of the Charleston had been abandoned, and it was simply known as the Quickstep, which would eventually become standardized.

The dance we know today owes a lot to an English chap called Wally Fryer. The old dance had swinging variations very much like a Waltz, with its spin turns, lock steps and double lock steps, but Fryer, who was a professional dancer and World Champion, decided to inject more excitement by adding step hops, scatter chassés, flickers, whipper taps and tricks into his routines. The footwork was quicker, more intricate and therefore much more interesting than it had been, and when he and his dancing partner Violet Barnes

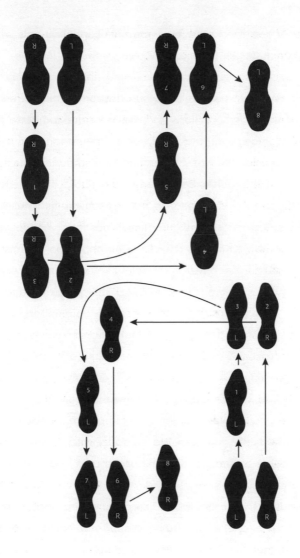

performed round the ballrooms of London it was an instant hit.

Old Wally was a remarkable quickstepper. He was a fast, light dancer who sped across the floor and yet danced with flamboyance and style, which is what this dance cries out for. He was also unbeatable when it came to dancing the Quickstep in competitions. But by the end of the forties Wally had decided to hang up his dancing shoes and retire from competitive dancing, though he still performed on the Park Lane hotel ballroom circuit. He passed his dancing mantle to Len Scrivener, an exceptional dancer. Len and his partner Nellie Duggan were widely considered to be strong competitors and very technical dancers. They had won many leading championships and were known for their prowess in the Tango. When Wally was on the scene and competing alongside Len you could guarantee that while Wally and Violet would always win the Quickstep heats, it would be Len and Nellie who took the Tango. And now, with Wally out of the picture, Len was the undisputed king of both.

Needless to say, that suited Len. Who doesn't want to be number one, after all? But then suddenly, much to Len's consternation, Wally decided to come out of retirement. A huge ballroom competition was being held – one that offered a very large purse of prize money – which was just too tempting for Wally to ignore. And so he dusted off his tail coat and with Violet in hold went head to head with Len once again. This was big news in the dance world. By the time they faced off in the final, the crowds went wild. At first they were cheering the current champion, Len, but as the heats went on it was Wally they were calling for as he dazzled with his Quickstep. This was a rumble in the ballroom jungle, and eventually it was Wally Fryer who took home the purse. After that display Wally went back into retirement, much to Len's relief.

The Quickstep is a tricky dance to master so take it slow at first – learn to walk before you fly. But if you do take it up, here's one piece of advice: this may not be one to try at home, unless you've suddenly taken up lodgings with the Queen. This dance requires movements on a grand scale and you don't want to end up with your partner's head on the ceiling and your leg stuck in the television set.

★ ★ ★

R IS FOR ...

REHEARSAL

Life may not be a dress rehearsal, but when it comes to ballroom dance rehearsal is what its all about. It's no good thinking that a few sequins and a full-on spray tan is going to give you what it takes to impress the judges when you hit the floor; you need practice, practice, practice. When it comes to working with me in the studio – to borrow a line from *Fame* – right here is where we start paying for it, in sweat.

In competition dancing you spend hours together in the studio – or wherever you can – going over those dances again and again, and then on the day of the competition you find yourselves on the ballroom floor rehearsing alongside the other couples … and that's when things can get a little fraught, as you size up the enemies and identify the ones to beat. Tense is not a word I would use to describe these rehearsals – instead, I'd say they were simply exasperating!

RISE AND FALL

This has nothing to do with the Roman Empire, some of you less scholarly types will be relieved to hear, and with any luck doesn't refer to my career either, for the moment at least. No, when we talk about rise and fall we are describing the movement of elevation created by the straightening of the legs. When we rise onto our toes we start to straighten our legs and stretch our bodies and heighten ourselves in the process, and then we immediately lower ourselves, falling into our starting position. Rise and fall is used to interpret musicality and you need good footwork and timing to do it properly. It's a movement that occurs in all of the standardized dances. In particular it is integral to the English Waltz, as when executed in a pronounced way it gives that dance its sense of elegance. The only dance in which it's not needed is the Tango, which is danced on the flat.

ROGERS, GINGER

It would be wrong to name-check Fred Astaire in this book without giving a nod to Ginger Rogers too. He performed alongside many wonderful dancers in the course of his career, but it was his partnership with Ginger that set the screens on fire. One could say that in Ginger, Fred had met his ultimate match: she could sing, she could act, she was a natural comedian and, boy, could she dance. She was born in 1911 and over the course of her career she made 73 films, winning an Academy Award for one. But it is the ten she made with Fred that she is best remembered for: *Top Hat*, *Roberta*, *The Gay Divorcee* and *Shall We Dance?* among them. They did much to revolutionize the screen musical genre.

Ginger's career began when she won a Charleston competition in her home town as a teenager. Broadway beckoned and she first met Fred when she was performing in a production of George and Ira Gershwin's *Crazy Girl*, which he had been hired to choreograph. This play made her a star overnight and it wasn't long before she was signed to the Hollywood studios and partnered with Fred.

What made Ginger such a great entertainer was that she had it all – the looks, the voice, the elegance – and as a dancer she was a natural. She was flexible, she was quick-footed and she was able to convey both character and emotion as she moved. She was also a hard worker, keeping up with the punishing rehearsals that Fred insisted on without complaint. He respected her for this, having worked with other actresses who wouldn't or couldn't put up with his perfectionism. As Fred once said of her: 'She made things very fine for both of us and she deserves most credit for our success.' Ginger Rogers was a match for any man and she knew it too, giving us the immortal line: 'I do everything the man does, only backwards and in high heels!'

RUMBA

The Rumba is the dance of love, so if you're in the mood to get up close and personal with your partner, take to the floor with this one. It's intimate, it's sensual and it's slow, so it gives you the time to get to grips with the dance itself – and also with your partner. But while this is the dance of love, it's not the dance of sex! It should be gentle and loving and all about longing. This isn't a one-night stand of a dance. It's about wooing the girl, taking her home, calling her the next day and introducing her to your mother the following week. It can be danced with a degree of fire and intensity but it should be endearing too, and at no time at all should it be vulgar. It's all about the eye contact and not about the fumble.

This dance really puts the Latino into Latin and you should aim to convey this when you perform it. Trussed up in a suitable Latin costume, you'll take to the floor to the sounds of a great South American number; one that's beautiful and romantic but has a certain amount of raunch to it. What I love about this dance is that it's all about the mood. It's all about intense love and the touch – and I do like a bit of touching, I can't deny it.

There are many forms of Rumba, but the standardized ballroom version hails from Cuba, where it was danced in the nightspots of Havana at the beginning of the last century. Alcedes Castellanos, a great Cuban bandleader at the time, took the dance to Paris in the twenties, but it was thanks to a dance teacher called Monsieur Pierre Margolie that we have it in the UK in its current form. Monsieur Pierre was responsible not only for introducing most of the Latin American dances to London, where he had a dance school, but also for noting down their techniques. It was on his travels to Cuba with his dance partner Doris Lavelle after the Second World War that he witnessed a new style of Rumba – the Systemo Cubana – being danced, with a straight-legged technique. He brought this new version back to Europe in the fifties, and it was this that evolved into the International Technique we have today.

The Rumba is the slowest of all the Latin dances, but don't be fooled into assuming that it's therefore the easiest, for it is actually one of the hardest to master. You need a good sense of rhythm, timing, muscle control,

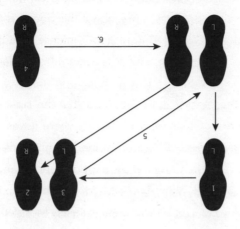

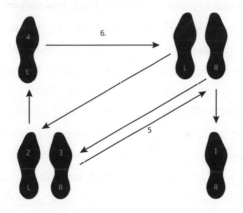

hip action and coordination; it's all about wriggling your hips rotationally and simultaneously bouncing on your feet. If you're the kind of person who finds it a challenge to rub your tummy and pat your head at the same time you might find this a bit of a challenge. But never fear you, will master it in the end!

Even I have had a few scrapes with the Rumba in the past, not least the time when I performed in a pair of trousers that were slightly too long. I was doing this wonderful step where I picked up my woman (in the dance that is, not at the bar afterwards) and dragged her backwards with her leaning on me. But as I did it I stood on the length of my trousers with my heel and slipped, with my foot going away from me. I ended up crashing onto the floor with her on top of me. That, I have to say, was not one of my finer moments. But I still love the Rumba.

S IS FOR ...

SALSA

There are two types of Salsa. There's the one you can eat along with your tortilla chips, and there's the one you can dance. Two entirely different entities, and yet what they have in common is that they are both rich in ingredients. As someone who has never learnt to cook I am not going to even attempt to tell you what's in the sauce, but what I can do instead is give you the recipe for the dance. So, to make the perfect Salsa we take a little Cha-cha-cha, and add in pinch of the Bossa Nova. We take the Mambo, which is danced on the 2/2 count, and speed it up to the 4/4 count. And then we season it with a lot of rotational hip action and some swivelly steps, just for good measure.

The Salsa is the mother of all Latin dances and probably the most popular. It's the one we all think we know, and (in some cases rather misguidedly) try to do. It looks easy enough to perform but you need to be nimble and have good balance. It's all about shifting your weight from one foot to another, and moving your hips round and round while keeping your upper body level as you move from open to closed positions, hand in hand. So it takes a lot of practice and coordination.

Now, I like the Salsa but I have a confession to make – I don't dance it very often, simply because I don't think I look very good doing it. I always look like a ballroom dancer doing Salsa, which bothers me. I think perhaps I am overly postured for it. I feel like I'm having a great time when I dance it and then look at myself and think 'no'. It's one of the dances that either comes naturally to you or it doesn't, in my view.

If you're going to try it then my tip is to get stuck in. You want to feel the emotion of the motion, really let go and get those hips going. You do have to be quite agile to salsa well and it's a difficult dance for a novice to master. Former cricketer Mark Ramprakash is a notable exception to the rule. He's proved himself to be a Salsa King, with more than enough hip!

SAMBA

I am going to transport you to Brazil for this dance. It's a warm, balmy evening, we are on the streets of Rio de Janeiro, the music is playing – and so what better way could there be to pass the time than to dance? And what does one dance in Brazil? The Samba, of course: the embodiment of that nation and its people. It's fun, it's lively, it's upbeat – an explosion of colour and rhythm. Think of headdresses, heels and skimpy little dresses, embrace the spirit of Mardi Gras, channel your inner Carmen Miranda (girls, not boys!) and let's get ready to party.

The Samba is one of the most exuberant of all the standardized Latin numbers. It's filled with energetic, vibrant movements and steps danced to a quick tempo and a strong rhythm. There is an 'anything goes' quality to the Samba, which makes it so much fun both to dance and to behold. But as carefree as the Samba might look, don't be lulled into a false sense of security, especially once fired up with a Caipirinha or two, for it is one of the most difficult of the Latin dances to master. You need both technique and a good sense of timing. It is also a progressive dance, which means you progress round the floor as in ballroom dance (the only other Latin dance in which this occurs is the Paso Doble), so you need direction.

The Samba is all about timing and changing rhythms, and this is where it gets complicated. You might have to brush up on your fractions here because it's all about dancing on split beats. So here's the technical

bit. The music for this dance is in 2/4 time, but that first beat is split into three-quarters of a beat, and a quarter of a beat. And then the second beat is a whole beat. Got that? No, I didn't think you would, so to spell it out in English it's a 'one-a-two', or three counts but two beats. If that all seemed a little technical, that's because it was. But what I am trying to demonstrate here is just how important it is to master the rhythm of the dance; if you can't nail that, you're just going to be bouncing around indiscriminately. Samba has a bounce to it, but it's a controlled bounce contained within the hips and the legs. We don't want you looking like you've arrived at the carnival or the dance floor on a space hopper.

Samba music itself combines three different cultures: there are strong African rhythms, Portuguese songs and fast-paced Indian rituals. All of which gives the dance its wonderfully exotic flavour. Various Samba styles have been danced for centuries. At first it was a simple dance that involved body rolls and sways, but as time went on carnival steps were added and by the nineteenth century it started to be danced in hold. The Zemba Quecca, as it was then known, was hugely popular among the high society of Rio and São Paulo, and as time went on it would merge with other dances such as the Mesemba and the Maxixe.

By the thirties Samba had become hugely popular around the world. The Parisians loved it – and so did us Brits, though we knew it then as the Carioca, and when in 1939 it was performed at the World Exhibition in New York ... well, we all went Samba mad. A flurry of Hollywood movies followed, with the Brazilian actress and singer Carmen Miranda starring in many, including the memorable *That Night in Rio*. Even Fred and Ginger got in on the act in *Fly Me Down to Rio*.

Samba is one of the most popular of all the ballroom dances and pupils keen to learn Latin always flock to these classes, but I can't over-emphasize how hard it is to master, because there is so much going on within the dance. You are trying to get some hip action going and achieve the correct amount of bounce, without being too bouncy ... I hated the Samba when I first started dancing it as a boy; I couldn't see the point of it. But in time, and after a lot of practice, I got the hang of it and when I did I loved it. When you do learn to do it properly you get a lovely rippling feeling as you dance, and you feel as if you are on casters as you glide across the floor.

Samba still has its place on the streets of Brazil, being the centrepiece of the annual carnival in Rio, where thousands of dancers, who have spent months rehearsing in their local Samba schools, take to the streets in their elaborate costumes. Now, you might not want to go for that scantily clad look with your feathers and headgear, especially on a wet night in Grimsby, but it's still a wonderful dance to try and learn.

SEPARATION

What I am doing here is standing in front of the bull, and appelling – stamping my foot on the ground to get the bull's attention. Then I make two steps towards the bull, air the cape, and in so doing I am tempting the bull … and fate. So this kind of separation is a variation in the Paso Doble, rather than a phase you go through when you and your dance partner decide to call time on your ballroom marriage.

SEX

Cover your eyes, children, because this entry might be a little too racy for you (which no doubt is going to encourage you to read on). 'Dancing is a perpendicular expression of a horizontal desire,' George Bernard Shaw once said, and I couldn't have put it better myself. Dancing is a very good way of girls and boys coming together, and let's be honest about it, that was the real reason why I took it up as a teenage boy. Who wants to spend their Tuesday night in the rain on the football pitch with a group of pimply lads when you can be surrounded by a bevy of delightful young ladies in dance class, all desperate for your attention, as you are the only chap in the room? It's a no-brainer, to me.

You can be very popular with the ladies if you dance well, boys – even if it's just in class. And if you make your partner look wonderful then she's going to love you all the more for it. But we want to keep it quite clean and not be lascivious or smutty in any way. As for you girls – men love a woman who can move well. It doesn't matter what you look like – if you can dance you will be a goddess in their eyes. Dancing is all about chemistry and allure, the promise of something to come, a big physical flirt off.

But, boys and girls, don't take things too far. Ballroom dance is a family affair and we don't want too much smut on the floor. If you feel that way, get a room. And when it comes to being sexy, try to do it naturally. Male dancers often get this wrong in my view; they try too hard, get all macho and end up looking like a seventies porn star when they dance. This is really frightening for the lady. You don't have to try to pretend to be a man because, without wanting to state the obvious, you are already a man, so just dance as yourself. And ladies, 'sexy' doesn't mean putting it all out there on show either. Sex appeal isn't about being revealing

– there are other forms of dance for that – it's about smouldering sensuality; the chase, the game. It's what I like to think of as floor play.

SPORTSMANSHIP

What I love about ballroom dance is that it brings people together, no matter who they are or where they come from. It can be enjoyed by peasants and royalty alike, with different styles being embraced around the world, and dances originating from an array of countries from Bavaria to Brazil.

But there have been periods in history when we haven't felt so friendly towards our foreign cousins, and one such incident that springs to mind took place at the end of the fifties. Wally Fryer and Violet Barnes had once again been crowned the British Champions, and as a result had been asked to celebrate at an event held at one of London's top hotels, with all the bigwigs from the ballroom world in attendance. A good time was being had by all, and after the speeches and toasts had come to an end an announcement was made. A special invitation had been made at the request of the official ballroom board in Tokyo for Wally and Violet to come to Japan and perform a demonstration held at an

Imperial dinner. It was an honour, indeed. This was the first time a pair of British Champions had been asked to dance at the Imperial Court, and so all the guests rose to their feet applauding Wally and Violet for this wonderful achievement. But I'm afraid Wally didn't see it that way. He stood up at the top table to say a few words, which everyone simply assumed would be of thanks, and let loose. 'If you think I'm going to Japan, you're wrong!' was the general gist of it. 'I'm not going to Japan because those sods shot my brother in the war!' Suffice to say, it was a rather awkward moment. The room fell silent, no one knew what to say, and Josephine Bradley reputedly choked on her champagne. Rightly or wrongly, Wally stuck to his guns and didn't take up the invitation. Len Scrivener and Nellie Duggan were sent instead. Needless to say, such a thing would never happen today.

SWAY

We can all sway a little when we have partaken of a drink or two, but when we talk about sway in ballroom it refers to a technique. A sway is simply an inclination of the body to the left or the right, either to add decoration or embellishment to a ballroom dance, or to regain balance where needed. If I am static and sway, then it's an adornment to a variation – adding a little bit of drama to a dance such as the Paso, giving a movement both line and a nice, finished look. But if I am moving and I sway then I am using this action as a natural counterbalancing movement – or CBM as we say in ballroom – to the movement I have just performed. It is the tipping of the body to one side or the other to balance the motion of the move. It is rather like motorcyclist taking a bend, only in ballroom we don't wear helmets – though if you are just starting out, perhaps you should.

If we didn't sway when we moved we would land flat on our faces, so you need to master the art. Sway doesn't start from the waist – it should start from the feet and involve the whole body and legs. It needs to look seamless and effortless, otherwise you'll just give the impression that you're about to keel over.

When done in perfect harmony a good sway can give quality to a dance routine. If, on the other hand, you are swaying before you've hit the dance floor because you've spent too long at the bar, take my advice and just go home.

TANGO

Earlier in the book we got to grips with the Argentine Tango, but now it is time to introduce the modern Tango, the one we dance in ballroom. It's a far more formal dance and has much more structure to it. Girls, you'll be relieved to hear that it is a lot less sweaty than the Argentine Tango (and no money is changing hands in this dance, either) and lads, you'll probably be disappointed to note that it's a little less raunchy. But that doesn't mean that the modern Tango lacks any of the passion or the heat of the Argentine. It's still dramatic, it's wonderfully exotic, madly intense and quite romantic, which is why I love this dance.

The ballroom Tango inherited much from its Argentine counterpart. We still have the passion and intensity between the man and the woman; we have its flicks, swivels and kicks; the closeness of the torsos − all the key components are there. But what makes this dance different is that we are dancing progressively round the floor, as we always do in ballroom but not necessarily in

Latin. And by doing that, essentially taking the Tango out of the bordello and onto the ballroom floor, the dance is given a more romantic feel and we have more of a love story.

So, to pull this dance off you and your partner must be in perfect harmony. The audience needs to feel that togetherness between you two for it to be convincing. I don't want to look at this dance and immediately realize that the pair of you met half an hour ago at the bus stop. I need to believe that you are a couple and in love, even if you aren't. Likewise, if you are together but are in the midst of some acrimonious split and heading off to the court of this-is-yours-and-that's-mine, then sit this one out too, because I don't want you using this as an excuse to repeatedly kick each other in the shins. There is a memorable line in the film *Scent of a Woman* when Al Pacino's character says 'If you get tangled up, just tango on ... ' – but to my mind if you get tangled up you're actually going to end up on the floor with your legs akimbo.

The Tango is about love and desire and that's what we need to see in the dance as the couple move round the floor together, swivelling and twining around one another. The Tango has a more intense style of hold than other dances. Here the man takes hold of his partner's

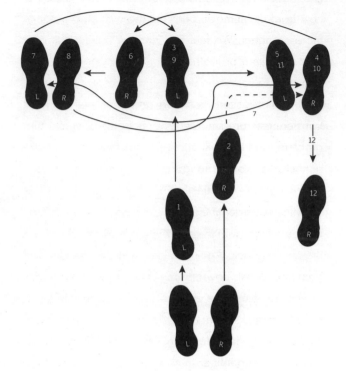

right hand, with her arm picked up to his eye level but bent in at the elbow so that the hands come towards the couple. The man should have his right arm round the lady's back but slightly lower than the shoulder blades. This allows her to place her left hand over and underneath the man's palm, facing down, rather than placing it on his arm. This already takes the dance to a new level of intimacy, because the partnership is much more compact. We feel that the man has gathered his lady up. Like it or loathe it, girls, in this dance it is time to give in to your man and let him take control and lead you. If his footwork is strong and sure and his weight transferences are smooth and correct you won't have a problem, and that will allow you the time to concentrate on the artistry of the Tango.

As with the Argentine Tango, contact between the two bodies is high, with the couple leaning into one another, their heads back. Again we have freedom of movement from the waist down, allowing for all the seductive swivels, turns and the entwinement of the legs and those flicks and tricks with the footwork. The music for the modern Tango is quite distinct and intricate, much more so than the Argentine, in which the tempo can be quite variable, and that's what gives the dance its punchy, staccato flavour.

I like to dance the Tango to traditional music, my favourites' being Jacob Gade's 'Tango Jalousie' or Gardo Matos Rodríguez's 'La Compasita'. You could dance it to something more contemporary, but make sure you have chosen a piece with not only the right tempo but the right flavour as well.

The Tango has been around for hundreds of years, but the modern version of the dance only really came to the fore at the start of the twentieth century, when it was danced in the clubs and ballrooms of Paris, Berlin, St Petersburg and New York. It came into fashion a year before the outbreak of the First World War, and by 1914 our American cousins had already developed a style of their own, the North American Tango.

We were dancing it in London by then too, but of course, being terribly British and frightfully polite about all things, our style of Tango was toned down, as it was deemed to be slightly too steamy. In 1921 the dance became standardized, and with the release of the silent movie *The Four Horsemen of the Apocalypse*, in which it was showcased by a smouldering Rudolph Valentino, the dance really found its footing around the world.

Come the thirties there was a further interpretation of the dance, thanks to a German couple who had arrived in London to demonstrate their new style. Having altered the timing of the dance, the Tango was no longer a smooth, slow number but became staccato and sharp. Into this they had incorporated new positions, which included longer leg strides for the dancers and different flicks and head positions for the lady, and overall the dance was more progressive. Aficionados of the old Tango gasped with disapproval, but only momentarily, for this was to become the Tango that we know today.

Someone once noted that the various forms of tango are like stages of a marriage. 'The American Tango is like the beginning of a love affair, when you're both very romantic and on your best behavior. The Argentine Tango is when you're in the heat of things and all kinds of emotions are flying: passion, anger, humour. The International Tango is like the end of the marriage, when you're staying together for the sake of the children.' Now, I'm not sure about that reference to the International Tango, because as far as I'm concerned any form of this dance should always be full of passion. So if it feels as if you are just staying there just for the kids, I'd divorce yourself from the Tango altogether.

TECHNIQUE

Technique is what makes dancing work. It's like a long equation of variables that when put together in a particular order not only makes a particular dance but distinguishes it from another. Back in the old days, we'd adopt the latest dance trend and interpret it as best we could, making it up as we went along. But in the twentieth century that started to change, and people began putting the dances down on paper and telling us what to do. There were many tomes of dance instruction published but perhaps the most famous of all was by a chap called Alex Moore, a champion ballroom dancer and competition adjudicator. Moore, the author of many other books on classical ballroom, here set about annotating all the steps and movements he saw performed by the best dancers of the day. He looked at what they should and shouldn't be doing, he theorized on what made certain dances work and, genius that he was, he put it all down on paper ... for it to become the source of the standardized technique that we still follow today.

I am a firm believer in technique, because without it ballroom just falls apart, and it was technique that first attracted me to ballroom dance (that and the girls). I loved the correctness of it all, the discipline and the form – and it's why I never liked disco, because it just seemed to be all over the place. I liked the fact that there were proper steps to learn, there was direction, a way of doing things and a structure. I like a good dose of heavy discipline – on the dance floor, that is.

★ ★ ★

TELEVISION

Television dance competitions have never been so popular. Tens of millions of people watch them around the world.

Why do we love these shows so much? In my opinion it's not just because we like dance. What makes them work is the fact that they put celebrities to the ultimate test – to try to do something difficult live on television. Every week we sit down and follow their trials and tribulations as they try to master a dance. From the comfort of our sofas we laugh at them when things go wrong, we cheer when they finally manage to get it right, marvel at their progress as the series moves on and root for our favourites on the night of the final. And during that time, whether we can dance or not, we all become armchair aficionados. Scoffing when the celebrity makes a false move, opining on whether a number was good or bad, audibly disagreeing with the judges when they make a criticism as we wave our imaginary paddles with our scores in the air. It is good old-fashioned entertainment at its best, and we all need a little dose of that from time to time.

Despite the increasing popularity of these shows I should point out that this is far from being a new phenomenon; in fact we have had something of a taste for them for quite some time. As far back as 1948, the BBC first broadcast a dancing programme called *Dancing Club*, which gave the viewers lessons in and demonstrations of ballroom dance. *Dancing Club* was actually a hybrid of a radio show that was broadcast at the start of the decade and was hosted by a wonderfully smooth chap called Victor Silvester. Silvester was a man of many talents. Not only was he a singer and a musician but he was also one of the most popular big band leaders of the time, so much so that during his career he sold a staggering 75 million records. He was also a great ballroom dancer, and did much in his lifetime to champion the artform.

So Silvester was the perfect choice to front *Dancing Club*, and in its original incarnation as a radio show millions of listeners would tune into their wirelesses each week to listen as he slowly and carefully dictated the steps to a dance routine. When the programme was televised at the end of the decade it became such a success that it stayed on our screens for another 17 years. Word has it that it was one of our late Queen Mother's favourite programmes, and as she sat down to watch it her young daughters – our current Queen Elizabeth and her sister Princess Margaret – would fly past the television screen as they practised the routines together.

On the back of the success of *Dancing Club* the BBC decided to introduce another ballroom dancing show into the schedule. First aired in 1949, *Come Dancing* was at first simply another dance instruction show broadcast from ballrooms around the United Kingdom, but in 1953 the format changed and it became a ballroom dance competition that pitted regions head to head against one another until it whittled them down to a winning couple. Hosted by the likes of Terry Wogan, Angela Rippon and Michael Aspel in its heyday, *Come Dancing* was a huge primetime draw.

In the eighties I appeared in an episode of *Come Dancing* but I have to admit that it was something of a disaster. The floor space was so small we could barely move, and the situation wasn't helped by the fact that the bandleader took it upon himself to pace up the music – and refused to slow down. So when we danced the Quickstep it was so quick that it was all we could do to stay focused. The evening's only consolation was that we were being adjudicated by one of the finest judges in the land – step forward Mr Len Goodman – in eighties suit and tie, large glasses … and looking rather youthful.

By the late nineties it seemed the general viewing public had tired of the programme (I hope my presence on the show didn't contribute to that) and it was axed in 1998.

It would be another six years before ballroom returned to our screens with the first series of *Strictly Come Dancing*. At the time perhaps no one could have imagined quite how popular the show would become. Today it's one of the most popular shows on British television, and has been joined by a number of other formatted dance shows on prime-time television.

Celebrities and amateurs alike who take part on these shows often describe it as like being part of a family, and that's one of the reasons I think they get so upset when they leave if they get voted out or don't get the points they need to stay on for the next round. And that family extends well beyond the studios, it includes all the passionate viewers. To me, they've helped put my beloved ballroom back on the map once more. I think we could all do with a little dancing to lift our spirits and bring a smile to our faces, especially in these difficult times.

TURNS

'The lady's not for turning,' Margaret Thatcher famously once said. Now Lady Thatcher might have been a great prime minister – depending on the sway of your politics – but with an attitude like that she would have made a lousy ballroom dancer, because turns crop up everywhere in this form of dancing. We have spin turns, pivot turns, reverse turns, natural spin turns, quarter turns and spot turns … I could go on, but even listing them is making me feel dizzy. The key to a well-executed turn is to lead well, follow through, and know when and where you are supposed to finish – which some might argue is a rule of thumb the Iron Lady might have adhered to in her own political career.

U IS FOR ...

UPPER BODY

I do like an upper body – or upper circumference, depending on your build – and one of the joys of my job is being allowed to go there. But, ladies and gentlemen, when you are presenting your upper torso to your partner, keep it nice. We want to see perfect form and we need flexibility, so relax into it and try not to be too stiff. And when we talk of presenting your upper body – don't read that as an invitation for a quick flash.

UNITY

Unity is what ballroom dance is all about – those two bodies coming together in perfect harmony and dancing together as one. When you perform together I never want to think of you as two separate entities. I want to see a whole and complete form.

But Unity in this context also refers to the society beauty and Nazi sympathizer Unity Mitford, who was, along with her equally famous sisters, a member of the Cavendish family and the daughter of the Duke of Devonshire. Born in 1914, Unity was something of a rebel as a young girl. It is said that when she 'came out' as a debutante at the age of seventeen in the thirties she tired of the constant litany of dances she was forced to attend. So in order to create a little mischief she would release her pet rat, Ratular, or her grass snake, Enid, onto the dance floor in order to 'liven things up a little'.

V IS FOR ...

VIENNESE WALTZ

The Viennese Waltz is the oldest of the standardized ballroom dances, but don't let that fool you into assuming that there is anything tame about this great granddame of the form. In its time it was regarded as being really rather louche. When we think of either of the Waltzes today we tend to think of them as elegant, rather refined dances: boys in tail coats, girls in flowing frocks dancing to beautiful music. But when the Viennese Waltz was first introduced to the United Kingdom in the early nineteenth century it scandalized society. It was regarded as shameless, brazen even, and no one could believe their eyes when they saw it performed for the first time. A man facing a woman in that way, his arm around her waist, like that, clasping her in what seemed to be the most intimate of embraces (and in public too!) as they rotated round the room. It was shocking! Miss Celbart, in her book on appropriate behaviour and social etiquette, deemed the Waltz 'a dance of too loose character for maidens to perform'. Even Lord Byron, who, with his penchant for the girls and his debauched and hedonistic lifestyle was hardly a saint himself, deemed it to be 'unchaste' and let his views be known in his poem 'The Waltz'.

Then came the Victorian age when everything was all very proper, so we could forgive them for a little pomposity – but the irony was that Queen Victoria, who was said to be a gifted ballroom dancer and rather nimble on those tiny feet of hers, loved the Waltz. She and Prince Albert liked nothing more than to practise in the privacy of their palaces when they had a night off. When news of this leaked, the dance became at once not only acceptable but hugely popular and everyone was at it, finding it rather fun to dance so closely together. What better argument for the survival of the monarchy? God bless the Queen, is what I'll say to that.

Now I'm all for a little excitement, but the thrill I get from dancing the Viennese Waltz isn't a cheap one, because I don't find anything particularly naughty in it. Instead the sense of exhilaration comes from the speed of the dance and from the continuous twirling and whirling round the floor. This is a fairground ride of a number. It's the fastest of all the ballroom dances – faster even than the Quickstep – and because of that most people feel quite dizzy when they first start dancing it. There isn't a single straight line in this dance, just a continuous succession

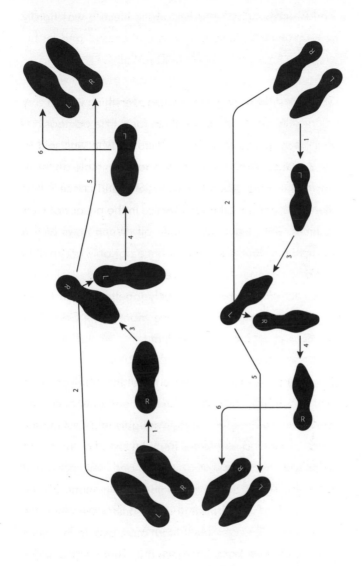

of fast turns as you move round the room making full use of the floor.

One might assume, given its name, that the Viennese Waltz had its origins in – well – Vienna, but there are many different theories as to how it first evolved, with half of Europe laying claim to it. In the twelfth century a form of Waltz called the Nachtanz was danced in Bavaria. Towards the end of the sixteenth century the French were performing a Volta to folk music. The Italians stake their claim as well, arguing that *volta*, which means to turn, is their word. Honestly!

They are all entitled to their opinions, of course, but as far as I'm concerned the closest relative of the Viennese Waltz is probably the Landler, danced in Austria in the eighteenth century. This wasn't a court dance though, far from it – it was a dance for us peasants. The nobility were appalled by the dance, deeming it to be lascivious because it allowed a sneaky peek of the lady's ankles. They even tried to have it banned but this just made it all the more popular, and it wasn't long before the posh lot started dancing it themselves. Thanks to the compositions of Josef and Johann Strauss and Josef Lanner the Austrians became a nation of Waltz lovers. Ornate dance halls such as the Zum Sperl starting popping up all over the city, and it wasn't long before the dance travelled round Europe, arriving in England in 1813. The Viennese Waltz has developed over the years and is now one of the most beautiful of all the ballroom dances. I urge you try it.

Thankfully, it has fewer steps to master than some of the other ballroom dances, which I realize may come as something of a relief. Instead it's all about grand turns and great big sweeping movements, so if you are going to attempt to try it at home you might want to move the furniture out of your sitting room and put the cat out. The things to concentrate on are your poise and the space between you and your partner – we don't want your heads banging together as you whizz round the room. The key is to build up to the top speed of the dance, otherwise you'll just keep chasing your tail on the spot or crashing into other couples on the floor. Take it slowly at first so you get used to it and overcome your dizziness. One of my partners really struggled with the dance – not technically, but simply because it made her feel like she was on a fairground ride, and she often wanted to throw up when we rehearsed it. I sympathized, for much as I like to get a little giddy, when I stop turning I would prefer it if the room around me did as well.

The Viennese Waltz is my kind of dance. I love the movement of the dance, its energy and the skill that's required for it. I adore all the classic tunes that work with it – 'The Blue Danube', 'The Minute Waltz'. And I love the frocks. But reader, fear not, tempted as I am, you'll only ever see me in a tail coat.

W IS FOR ...

WALK

I know what you're thinking: why on earth has he included a section on walking when this is a book about the art of ballroom dancing? If we didn't know how to put one foot in front of the other, we'd hardly be attempting to chassé, would we? Well, let me explain. Walking is an integral part of ballroom dance, or any form of dance for that matter, and unless you can get this right it's all going to go very, very wrong.

Now I know you all know how to walk, but 'the walk' in dance terms is very different from the one you do as you take a casual stroll down the high street with your shopping. The walk here is all about beautiful posture, transference of weight and timing. I don't expect you to walk this way in everyday life, otherwise you'll look rather poncy (and I should know), but I always want to see you move this way on the dance floor because it will give you both style and grace. It will also give you a sense of purpose, as if you know what you are doing – which helps.

Start with your feet closed and your weight equally balanced between them. Your knees should be slightly flexed, and you then start to move forward with your body as you step forward with the ball of the foot. As you slightly skim the floor with that moving foot you go onto your heel, and as you do that the heel of the supporting foot releases. See what you have there? Perfect weight transference and also timing, and that's what you are trying to achieve. Your weight is now central on both feet (on the heel of one foot and the ball of the other) and then passes through as your front foot flattens, thus taking the weight of your body. The back foot is pulled up from the toe, then the ball of the foot and then flattens as it passes the standing foot.

That might all sound simple enough, but remember that you have to do this backwards as well, without falling over! So for the backwards walk you start in the same position, feet together, knees flexed – equal weight on each foot. Your leg is swinging backwards – not from the knee but from the hip, otherwise you'll look like a crane – and this swing extends right down to the tip of your toe. Move the weight of this leg onto the ball of the foot, with your body weight remaining on the front foot. You need to master weight transfer here: as you start to transfer it your weight rolls from the toe to the back foot on the ball, while at the same time releases both the toe and the ball of the front foot. Your front leg should be straight now, your back knee slightly flexed. Your weight now passes through the central position on the heel of your front foot and the ball of your back. The heel of the front is drawn very lightly towards the back, skimming across the floor, and you should only lower the heel of the back foot when your front foot, which should be flat, passes beneath you.

Are you still standing? I hope so. Otherwise any dance you perform will at best look plodding and at worst won't be going anywhere, because it won't have the necessary movement. So, as I say to all my pupils, don't learn to dance before you can walk.

WALTZ (ENGLISH)

In ballroom there are two kinds of waltz: the Viennese, which we talked about earlier, and the English. While they are both rotational dances they are very different, and it's very important not to confuse them, especially when you take to the floor, because you'll look like a right wally if your partner does one thing and you do another.

The English Waltz has its origins in the Viennese and came onto the scene much later on, in the twenties. It retains the turns and the spins of the Viennese, but this is a much slower dance — half the tempo, in fact. It's all about big swinging sways and the accentuated rises and falls that give the dance its wonderful feel. It's a classic dance, full of grace and elegance — but despite having a history, it is not old-fashioned and actually quite modern. Gosh, I could have been describing myself there …

This is a big dance, fun to choreograph because you can throw so much into it — the spins and the turns — and we want to see all of this on a grand scale. It can be a hard dance to choreograph well, because what you want to achieve is that beautiful yet effortless sense of rise and fall throughout. In my opinion when it comes to the Waltz there are few better at it than my girl Erin, and she's simply stunning to watch when turning the floor in a handsome man's arms ... though I'd like to think that she enjoys dancing it with me as well.

The English Waltz we dance today is also known as the Diagonal Waltz because – you've guessed it – it is danced on the diagonal line. When we started waltzing over here there were two styles – the Diagonal, which was new, and the older rotary style – so everyone was getting a trifle confused as to which style of Waltz they should be dancing. Fashion and trends kept changing and it became a bit of a conundrum. However, the problem was solved in 1927 when the ISTD stepped in. They were looking to standardize the dance and so it was decided that whichever style of Waltz won the annual Star Championships (one of the most important dance competitions of the time) would become the official standardized English Waltz. And of course it was the Diagonal Waltz, performed by the magical dancing team of Phyllis Haylor and Alex Miller, which won the day – and the rotary was confined to history.

In the English Waltz you start by facing diagonally to the wall and move from there, and what happens with the alignment is that you end up with a much more expansive swinging Waltz then you would if you were following a rotational alignment. You take a forward step, then a

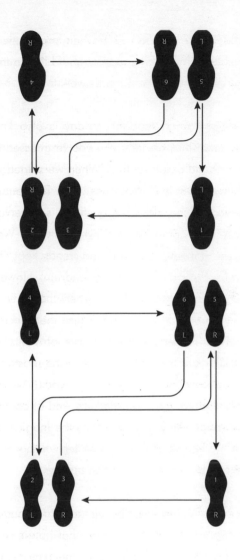

step to the side, and close your feet and you're away. The steps are fairly simple but you want neat footwork, so it's all about correct heels and toes. So, when you perform a Waltz, you start from the floor up. This, along with timing, will give you a beautiful rise and fall, a softness of swing, pivoted spins and effortless yet grand sways. And with any luck, starting from the floor will stop you slipping and sliding all over the place, because remember, you're dancing on the ballroom floor, not on ice.

WAR

'With the rage of war, comes the rage of dancing,' as Josephine Bradley noted in her memoirs *Dancing Through Life*, and we always take heed of everything Bradley says because she was the First Lady of Ballroom. An exquisite dancer and a gifted teacher, Bradley didn't just know about ballroom, she practically invented the form, having been one of first members of the board of the ISTD that standardized the first dances.

Anyway, I digress. We went through gloomy times during the First World War and yet we never stopped dancing. With so many young men being sent away, not knowing whether they would survive the battlefield, both they and their sweethearts indulged in nightlife for respite when they were on leave. Dressed in their uniforms, with women in full evening dress, they would dance the nights away to the popular tunes of the time such as 'If You Were the Only Girl in the World' and 'Tipperary'. Dancing had never been so popular, but then war and dancing have always had something of a history. Back in 1815, on the eve of the Battle of Waterloo, the Duchess of Richmond threw what has been described as the 'greatest ball in history' at her residence in Brussels. Every high officer in Wellington's army was there – as well as the great man himself – and they danced until dawn, when the officers slipped away to take their places on the battlefield. According to legend some of the officers were left with no time to change into their uniforms and so went onto the field in evening dress.

The years between the First and the Second World Wars were a significant time for dance too, for after emerging from the horrors of war there was a pervading spirit of gaiety and abandon. People started to embrace new styles of dance and music, societal mores loosened and inhibitions went out the window – especially on the ballroom floor.

In 1939, as the Second World War loomed, things closed down again as the country braced itself for what was coming next. And yet dancing was still never far from our minds. Even though the hotel ballrooms and dance halls closed, we still found places to dance, creating makeshift dance halls in the bunkers and air raid shelters round London, moving bunks and beds against the wall so there was room to dance.

Phyllis Haylor, who like Josephine Bradley was a doyenne of dance, being both a champion dancer and a highly respected teacher, writes poignantly of that time. Doing her bit for the war effort she had gone to work first as a driver for the Kensington ARP and later as a ministerial clerk. But she was desperate to teach again and so in the final year of the war she set up a dance class in an underground shelter. But it wasn't just those left here in Britain who missed their nights at the ballroom. The soldiers sent away to defend our land and fight for Queen and country obviously did too. In the midst of the war Haylor received a letter from a soldier. She didn't know the man in question, but he had found her address. He wrote to ask her whether ballroom dancing had changed in any way since he had been away. History doesn't relate whether he returned home safely or was ever able to dance again.

Now that we are no longer living in the shadow of the Blitz, or waiting for our dance partners to be sent away to the Front, it is hard to equate the froth and the feathers of the dance floor with such hard times. But it is worth remembering what dancing meant to people in wartime, and how they tripped the light fantastic to find a small escape from reality. Glamour, silks, satins and dance steps can mean so much more than a frivolous night out.

WEAVE

Just so you know, if I suggest that you try out a weave, I'm talking about you sitting down at a loom. A weave in dance is a variation you need to master for the Waltz. You commence from the Promenade Position, facing diagonally to centre, and as you fulfil the required steps you should end either in a closed position or back in the Promenade.

WEIGHT CHANGE

Weight change is key to any form of dance, but before you all start jumping on the scales, signing up for the gym or putting yourself on some punishing diet, hold on! I'm not sizing up your waistlines or wobbly bits here; instead I am talking about the transference of weight from one foot to another. Now that might sound simple enough – after all, if we didn't change our weight from one foot to another we'd remain static – but it's actually a skill that a lot of people find difficult to execute properly when they are learning to dance.

What you need to learn is how to transfer weight properly so that it looks graceful and seamless rather than clunky. Once you've mastered that you'll have balance, movement and with any luck you'll also be dancing in time. The key thing about weight change is to understand that we are always moving forwards even when we are going backwards. When travelling forwards the weight of the body should be forwards, but likewise when travelling sideways or backwards. Try not to split your weight between your two feet when dancing, because the elegance and grace of dance comes from having your weight on one foot at a time and transferring it with each step you perform.

On top of all this, there are variations of changing weight: part, half and full weight change. If you can do all of that, either naturally or through practice, then you're halfway to becoming quite a good little dancer. Once you've cracked it, you can start adding layers of technique on top, such as sway and sweeping movements. If you can't master weight change then keep trying, otherwise you're just going to look as if your feet have stuck to a large sheet of flypaper.

WHIP

The whip in ballroom isn't something that's hung in your stable – or even your bedroom for that matter. It's just nice little variation that occurs in the Jive.

WHISK

Likewise, a whisk isn't a kitchen implement but a variation featured in the Waltz. Furthermore, it doesn't take its name from that tool but instead from a tipple. Legend has it that there was a famous dance teacher who couldn't get through a class without having a glass of whisky in his hand (I know that feeling well, but thankfully I don't drink). He was in the midst of showing his pupils a reverse spin when he went off balance, popped his feet in another direction, and lo and behold a new variation – the whisk – was born.

X FACTOR, THE

Apparently this is a singing competition on a Saturday night. Never heard of it.

YANKS

Yanks, in this case, refers to the American GIs who were stationed here during the Second World War. We have a lot to thank them for, and I'm not just talking about the incredible contribution they made to the war effort. As well as that valiant gesture they gave us new music and new dances, importing swing and jazz to these shores and teaching us Brits the latest dance trends from across the pond. If it wasn't for them we would probably all still be doing the Waltz rather than the Jive.

Z is for ...

ZIGZAGGING

When we talk about Zigzagging in ballroom, we are actually referring to an old variation that was devised and danced in the thirties by the British ballroom champion and authority on technique, Henry Jacques. The variation has evolved over time but basically it goes step, step, behind step, forward step, as your feet zigzag. That's a technical description of a lovely variation.

But also, the word zigzag might take us right back to the beginning, because if you still haven't got to grips with your alignment and direction you are probably zigzagging all over the dance floor. And that of course is something we don't want to see: ballroom is all about fun and frolics, but it is also about beauty and harmony. And I hope that this book has given you a sense of how to get there.

EXIT

Ladies and gentlemen, we are finally reaching the end of our dance through the wonderful world of ballroom together, so it is time to make those final steps, add that little bit of flourish and give our routine a sense of an ending before we leave the dance floor. The music has stopped, the lights are up, the applause (or booing) has faded and together we wait in anxious anticipation as the judges make their final deliberations.

Together you and I have waltzed through the history of ballroom dance; we've foxtrotted our way through the formal standard ballroom numbers and hip-swivelled and sashayed through the Latin dances. We've donned Lycra and tails and transported ourselves to Rio and Buenos Aires, and then back to Blackpool (with a little bit of a thud, I grant you).

So, we've had to get a little technical at times and to learn a few movements and terms that we've struggled with as we journeyed round the dance floor – in the right direction, I hope. And there were moments when we might have got a little intimate in some of our holds. But I hope that we've had some fun and entertainment in the process because that, to me, is the whole point of ballroom dance. It's not about the marks, the prizes, the trophies or even the glitter balls (believe me!). It's all about having a big, energetic, sequin-filled blast of fun, no matter how good or bad you are as a dancer.

Born with two left feet? No problem, we'll adapt the steps for you. Got no sense of rhythm? Then we'll find you a partner who has and can lead you. Worried about how you might look in Lycra? Fear not, it's the answer to most of our prayers, as it holds everything in. Dance really is for everyone. It's the most wonderful way of meeting people, and a fun way of staying in shape (I'd much rather spend an hour on the dance floor with some lovely lady than sweating it out on the treadmill on my own in the gym). And above all it is hugely entertaining to watch. So, even if you are glued to your sofa and have no intention of ever reaching for your dancing shoes, please embrace ballroom dance with the type of passion and gusto you would your partner in a Tango. At the very least it will bring a smile to your face, and maybe with a bit of luck a slight tap to the sole of your foot.

And now that we've taken this brief excursion together into the wonderful, sparkly and exciting world of ballroom, I hope you will dance on. But before you do, ladies and gentlemen, let's just pause for a moment, move out of hold and hand in hand take our place on the dance floor, because I understand that the judges' scores are in ...